God's Word
On Divine
Healing

Kenneth E. Hagin

Unless otherwise indicated, all Scripture quotations in this volume are from the *King James Version* of the Bible.

Third Printing 2004

ISBN 0-89276-069-9

In the U.S. write:
Kenneth Hagin Ministries
P.O. Box 50126
Tulsa, OK 74150-0126
1-888-28-FAITH
www.rhema.org

In Canada write:
Kenneth Hagin Ministries
P.O. Box 335, Station D,
Etobicoke (Toronto), Ontario
Canada, M9A 4X3

Contents

Contents

Healing:
God at Work

Bible Texts: John 14:9,10; Acts 10:38;
Mark 16:15,17,18; James 5:14,15

Central Truth: If you want to see God at work,
look at Jesus — He's the will of God in action!

Some Christians who need healing have said to me, "Maybe God put this sickness on me for some purpose."

Did Jesus ever put sickness on anyone? When people came to Him for healing, did He ever turn even one away saying, "No, it's not My will. Just suffer a little longer. You're just not pious enough"?

No! Not once!

And the Scriptures tell us that to see God, we look at Jesus. Jesus Himself said:

JOHN 14:9,10
9 ... Have I [Jesus] been so long time with you, and yet hast thou not known me, Philip? he that hath seen me hath seen the Father; and how sayest thou then, Shew us the Father?

10 Believest thou not that I am in the Father, and the Father in me? the words that I speak unto you I speak not of myself: but the Father that dwelleth in me, he doeth the works.

God at Work

Do you want to know what God is like? Look at Jesus. Do you want to see God at work? Look at Jesus. Do you want to know the will of God? Look at Jesus. Jesus is the will of God in action (John 6:38). Did Jesus go about making people sick? No! He went about doing good and healing!

ACTS 10:38
38 How God anointed Jesus of Nazareth with the Holy Ghost and with power: who went about doing good, and healing all that were oppressed of the devil ....

From the natural standpoint, it is difficult for people to understand that most of the laws governing this earth today came into being through the fall of man — when Adam sinned and the curse came upon the earth. Because people don't understand this, they accuse God of accidents, sickness, and the death of loved ones. And God is not the author of any of these things.

People also blame God for the storms, catastrophes, earthquakes, and floods that occur. Even insurance policies call these "acts of God." No, they are not acts of God. They are acts of the devil. Their author is Satan.

All of these natural laws as we understand them were set aside by Jesus, whenever necessary, in order to bless humanity. Bear in mind that Jesus said, "He that has seen Me has seen the Father" (John 14:9). Well, we don't see Jesus bringing any storms on people. We see Him *calming* the storms!

Rebuker of Storms

A storm had arisen on the Sea of Galilee and Jesus was in the back of the ship asleep on a pillow. The disciples awoke Him and said, "Master, carest Thou not that we perish?" They thought they were going down at sea. But Jesus arose and *rebuked* the wind. He wasn't rebuking something God did. He was rebuking something the devil had stirred up.

You see, Adam was originally the god, so to speak, of this world. God made the world and the fullness thereof (Ps. 89:11). Then He made man, Adam. He said to Adam, "I give you the authority to rule this earth. You are the one who dominates." But Adam sold us all out to the devil. (He didn't have the *moral* right to do it, but he had the *legal* right, because the earth was his — God put it into his hands.)

Adam committed high treason and sold out to the devil. And the Bible tells us that now Satan is the god of this world (2 Cor. 4:4). When did Satan become the god of this world? After Adam sinned.

Under Control?

We need to get some of these things straight in our minds, because many in the church world are confused. People have all kinds of unscriptural ideas. Some think, *Well, God's got everything under control.* But that may or may not be so, according to how you mean it. If you mean that God is ruling the earth right now — no, He isn't! He's going to rule it again one of these days, but He's not right now.

During the Korean conflict, I read an article by a well-known newspaper columnist. He said, in effect, "I

2

don't claim to be a Christian, but I'm not an atheist or an agnostic. The atheist says there is no God. I believe there is one. The agnostic says there may be a God; he doesn't know. I believe there is.

"I don't believe everything just happened into being," he continued. "I believe some Supreme Being created everything. But what hinders me from being a Christian is what I hear preachers saying. I'm confused because they say God is running everything. And if He is, He sure has things in a mess."

Then the man alluded to wars, children being killed, poverty, disease, and sickness, saying, "I believe that there is a Supreme Being somewhere and that everything He made was beautiful and good. I just can't believe those things are the work of God."

Well, the truth is, those things came with the Fall when Adam sinned and Satan became the god of this world. When Satan is finally eliminated from the earth, there will be nothing that will hurt or destroy. And then it ought to be obvious where all those things came from.

Jesus' statement, "He that hath seen Me hath seen the Father," and His description of the Father make it impossible to accept the teaching that sickness and disease are from God. The very nature of God refutes such an idea, for God is love.

Let's go back to Acts 10:38 for a moment. Who anointed Jesus of Nazareth? God did! And Jesus said, "... the Father that dwelleth in me, he doeth the works" (John 14:10).

How did God do these works of healing through Jesus? By anointing Him with the Holy Ghost and with healing power. What did Jesus do with the anointing with which God had anointed Him? He went about doing good! What was the good that He did? Healing! So God was healing when Jesus healed, because it was God who anointed Him.

God is in the healing business, not in the sickness business! God is in the delivering business, not in the bondage business!

Jesus Healed All

Notice in Acts 10:38 who was healed by Jesus: "... ALL that were oppressed of the devil...." Now, that's a plain statement — all. *A-l-l!* That means everyone who was healed under the ministry of Jesus was oppressed of the devil. In other words, the devil had something to do with their sickness. That doesn't mean an evil spirit was always present. It just means the devil was behind the whole situation. They were oppressed of the devil — every one of them.

Yet to hear some people talk nowadays, even ministers, you would be led to believe that God and the devil had swapped jobs for the last 2,000 years! You'd think God was putting sickness on people and the devil was healing them. No, the devil is the same devil he always was. And God is still the same God.

MARK 16:15,17,18

15 And he [Jesus] said unto them, Go ye into all the world, and preach the gospel to every creature. . . .
17 And these signs shall follow them that believe; In my name shall they cast out devils. . . .
18 . . . they shall lay hands on the sick, and they shall recover.

Let's stop and analyze this. Which one of the sick did Jesus say to lay hands on? He just said *the sick*, period. Well, if God were the author of sickness, if He did put sickness and disease on people, and if it were His will for some to be sick, then this statement would be confusing — because Jesus authorized us to lay hands on *all* the sick and said they would recover.

If it were God's will for some to remain sick, Jesus would have had to say something like, "Lay your hands on those whom it is the will of God to heal, and they shall recover. And those whom it *isn't* God's will to heal, they won't recover." But that wasn't

the case. God set the Church against sickness, period!

JAMES 5:14,15

14 Is any sick among you? let him call for the elders of the church; and let them pray over him, anointing him with oil in the name of the Lord:
15 And the prayer of faith shall save the sick, and the Lord shall raise him up; and if he have committed sins, they shall be forgiven him.

Verse 14 asks, "Is *any* sick among you?" Among whom? The Church. So it must be God's will to heal any of the sick in the Church. Therefore, it can't be the will of God for "any" in the Church to stay sick.

Suffering With Jesus

"Brother Hagin," one individual said, "you've forgotten that the Bible said, 'If we suffer with Him, we'll reign with Him.'" No, I haven't forgotten. Let's look at that verse. *"If we SUFFER, we shall also reign with Him. . ."* (2 Tim. 2:12). Suffer what? Pneumonia? Cancer? Tuberculosis? No! What did Jesus suffer? Persecution! And you will too, if you live right.

You'll suffer persecution if you preach divine healing, the gifts of the Spirit, and faith. I've suffered persecution for preaching the Word in these areas. But I haven't suffered sickness and disease.

Another person said to me, "You've forgotten something else."

"What did I forget?" I asked.

"Why, right over there in the Book of Hebrews it says, 'Whom the Lord loveth He chasteneth'" (Heb. 12:6).

No, I didn't forget. That's still in there. But it doesn't say whom the Lord loveth *He makes sick*. You see, people have just put their own interpretation on that verse.

The word "chasten" in the Greek means *to child train* or *to educate*. You train your children, don't you? And you send them to school to be educated. But have you ever told a teacher, "If my child doesn't do right, knock his eye out"? Have you ever said, "If he is disobedient, break his leg" or "Give him cancer"? No! That isn't the way you discipline or train a child. And that's not the way God does it.

Job's Problems

God doesn't use sickness and disease to teach His children a lesson.

"But God made *Job* sick," someone said.

No, He didn't. The devil did.

"Yes, but God gave the devil permission."

True, but God didn't *commission* it. You see, God will permit you to rob a gas station, but He won't *commission* you to do it.

No, the Bible is plain about why sickness came upon Job. Job had said, ". . . *the thing which I greatly feared is come upon me, and that which I was afraid of is come unto me*" (Job 3:25). So he himself had opened the door to the devil by being afraid.

Bible scholars agree that the entire Book of Job took place in 9 to 18 months. And in chapter 42, you can read about the works of God! For example, Job 42:10 says that God turned Job's "captivity." That means when Job was sick, he was in captivity to the devil. When he was in poverty, he was in captivity to the devil.

But *God turned Job's captivity* and gave him twice as much as he had to begin with (v. 10)! Job lived 140 years after he got healed! That's God's work!

Paul's Thorn

"Don't you remember, though, that Paul was sick all his life, Brother Hagin."

No, I don't remember that. And you don't either.

"But he had a thorn in the flesh."

Where did you ever read in the Bible that a thorn in the flesh is sickness? Nowhere. Go back to the Scrip-

5

tures and see how that term is used. In the Old Testament, God said to Israel, "If you don't kill those Canaanites when you possess the land, they will be thorns in your side They will torment you" (Num. 33:55; Joshua 23:13; Judges 2:3).

Paul tells exactly what the thorn was — the messenger of Satan sent to buffet him (2 Cor. 12:7). Everywhere Paul went to preach, this evil spirit stirred up everything he could. He buffeted Paul in the flesh. And Paul couldn't command him to leave the earth, because he has a right to be here until Adam's lease runs out.

You can't separate sickness and disease from Satan. Disease came with the fall of man. The Fall was of the devil. Sickness and sin have the same origin — the devil.

Jesus' attitude toward sickness was an uncompromising warfare with Satan. His attitude toward sin and sickness was identical. He dealt with sickness the same way He dealt with demons. Since sickness and disease are of the devil, we must follow in the footsteps and attitude of Jesus and deal with disease as Jesus dealt with it.

✳

Memory Text:

"Verily, verily, I say unto you, He that believeth on me, the works that I do shall he do also; and greater works than these shall he do . . . ."

— John 14:12

Healing:
The Father's Provision

Bible Texts: Exodus 15:26; 23:25,26;
Deuteronomy 7:13-15; Psalm 103:3-5; 107:17-20

Central Truth: Everything connected with the
Body of Christ — the New Testament Church —
should bear the stamp of prosperity,
success, healing, surplus, and health.

God always has been opposed to sickness, not in favor of it. Even in the Old Testament, He always made provision for His covenant people to be healed. If sickness was His will, He wouldn't have made that provision.

When Israel crossed the Red Sea and started toward their homeland, the Lord said:

EXODUS 15:26
26 ... If thou wilt diligently hearken to the voice of the Lord thy God, and wilt do that which is right in his sight, and wilt give ear to his commandments, and keep all his statutes, I will put [literal Hebrew, "I will permit"] **none of these diseases upon thee, which I have brought** [permitted] **upon the Egyptians: for I am the Lord that healeth thee.**

Notice He isn't the Lord who made them sick. He said, "I am the Lord that *healeth* thee." God didn't put diseases upon Israel, nor upon the Egyptians. It is Satan, the god of this world, who makes man sick. Jehovah declares that He is Israel's Healer.

EXODUS 23:25,26
25 And ye shall serve the Lord your God, and he shall bless thy bread, and thy water; and I will take sickness away from the midst of thee.
26 There shall nothing cast their young, nor be barren, in thy land: the number of thy days I will fulfil.

As long as Israel walked in the Covenant, there was no sickness among them. There is no record of a premature death — no babies, young

7

people, or middle-aged people dying. With sickness taken away from the midst of them, the children of Israel lived out their lives without disease. They just fell asleep. When the time came for them to go, they would lay hands on their children and pronounce blessings upon them. Then they would gather their feet up into bed, give up the ghost, and go home.

"What does that have to do with us?" someone asked. "That was back then."

Well, God is the same God now as He was then. The Bible says He doesn't change (Mal. 3:6). God was against sin in the Old Testament, and He is against sin in the New Testament. He was against sickness in the Old Testament, and He is against sickness in the New Testament. He made provision for healing in the Old Testament, and He made provision for healing in the New Testament.

Deuteronomy 7:13 says, *"And he* [God] *will love thee . . . ."* Love thee! Love thee! Love thee!

But some people must not be reading the same Bible. They read, "And He will put sickness upon you and cause some of you to be stillborn and some of you to die when you're babies and some of you to be sick and crippled all your life. . . ."

No! No! No! That's not the Holy Scriptures. Here is the Word of God:

DEUTERONOMY 7:13-15

13 And he will love thee, and bless thee, and multiply thee: he will also bless the fruit of thy womb, and the fruit of thy land, thy corn, and thy wine, and thine oil, the increase of thy kine, and the flocks of thy sheep, in the land which he sware unto thy fathers to give thee.

14 Thou shalt be blessed above all people: there shall not be male or female barren among you, or among your cattle.

15 And the Lord will take away from thee all sickness, and will put [permit] **none of the evil diseases of Egypt, which thou knowest, upon thee . . . .**

"But that promise is not for us today, Brother Hagin," somebody said.

Are you sure? First Corinthians is in the New Testament, isn't it? Well, First Corinthians 10:11 says, *"Now all these things happened unto them* [Israel] *for ensamples* [examples or types]: *and they are written FOR OUR ADMONITION . . ."*!

Examples for Us

Glory! Deuteronomy 7:13-15 was written for my benefit! I think the Holy Spirit knew there would be those who would jump up and say, "That's just for the Jews. It's not for us!" So He wrote that what happened to them happened as examples to us. Those things "written aforetime,"

8

talking about the Old Covenant, were written for our learning (Rom. 15:4). Deuteronomy 7:13-15 was written for my admonition!

Do you think those people back then would be more blessed than the Church of the Lord Jesus Christ? Do you think they could be blessed financially and could prosper and be well, but the Church couldn't? Do you think that the Church — the Body of Christ, the Body of the Son of God, the Body of the Beloved — would have to struggle through life poverty-stricken, sick and afflicted, emaciated, and wasted away with starvation, singing, "Here I wander like a beggar through the heat and the cold"? No! That's not us!

We're Not Beggars

The Bible says we are joint-heirs with Christ, sons of God! We're not beggars! We're new creatures, blessed above all people!

You can see from the Scriptures that it was God's plan for everything connected with Israel to bear the stamp of prosperity and success. Disease and sickness were not to be tolerated among the Israelites, so the Church shouldn't tolerate sickness and disease either. Everything connected with the Body of Christ — the New Testament Church — should bear the stamp of prosperity, success, healing, surplus, and health.

What God said concerning Israel, He said in so many words concerning the Church. Romans 1:16 says, *"For I am not ashamed of the gospel of Christ: for it is the power of God unto salvation . . . ."*

I don't agree with all of Dr. Scofield's notes in his Reference Bible, but as a Greek and Hebrew scholar, his footnote on this verse in reference to the word "salvation" is excellent. He says, "The Greek and Hebrew words translated salvation imply the ideas of deliverance, safety, preservation, healing, and health."

Glory to God! The Gospel of Jesus Christ is the power of God unto *deliverance*! It is the power of God unto *safety*! It is the power of God unto *preservation*! And it is the power of God unto *healing* and *health*!

God Was Israel's Healer

The Psalms were Israel's prayer and song book, and they continually mention that God was Israel's Healer. Psalm 103 is a classic example.

PSALM 103:3-5
3 Who [the Lord] forgiveth all thine iniquities; who healeth all thy diseases;
4 Who redeemeth thy life from destruction; who crowneth thee with lovingkindness and tender mercies;

5 Who satisfieth thy mouth with good things; so that thy youth is renewed like the eagle's.

Disease came to Israel through disobedience of the Law. So forgiveness for their disobedience meant healing of their diseases.

After God told Israel that the reason for their sickness and disease was that they had rebelled against His words and against the counsel of the Most High (Ps. 107:11), He said:

PSALM 107:17-20
17 Fools because of their transgression, and because of their iniquities, are afflicted.
18 Their soul abhorreth all manner of meat; and they draw near unto the gates of death.
19 Then they cry unto the Lord in their trouble, and he saveth them out of their distresses.
20 He sent his word, and healed them, and delivered them from their destructions.

You see, the children of Israel took themselves out from under the protection of their covenant by wrongdoing. Well, we have a New Covenant. The Bible says that it's better than the Old Covenant (Heb. 8:6). And we too have divine protection. But it is possible to take ourselves out from under the protection of this covenant.

I'm not judging you. I'm judging me. I learned the truth years ago as a teenage boy on the bed of sickness. I was raised up after sixteen months of being bedfast: I was healed of two serious organic heart conditions, an incurable blood disease, and almost total paralysis. In the years following, the only time some physical disorder touched me was when I got out from under the protection — from under the cover. And, brother, I got back under it in a hurry!

When I say I got from under the cover, I don't mean that I stole something or told a lie on somebody. I just wasn't obeying God as I should. Perhaps He said to do something, or He told me to minister a certain way, and I went ahead and ministered the way I'd learned to minister instead of the way He said to minister. So I had to repent and get back in line. And the minute I did, I was immediately all right again physically.

For more than fifty years I haven't even had a headache. I've walked in health. And I'm not planning on being sick — I could be, but I'm planning on obeying God until I die. If Jesus tarries, I don't mind telling you that I'll live to a great age. I'll know before I go, and I'll tell everybody good-bye before I leave. I'll look over on the other side and say, "There it is, folks!" And then I'll be gone! I want to leave everyone shouting and happy, because that's the way I'm going.

"But Brother Hagin, you can't ever tell."

Oh, yes, you can tell. You can have exactly what God said you can have!

We have a better covenant than Israel had. If it was God's plan for the Israelites to live out their full length of time without sickness (who, by the way, were servants and not sons, under a covenant not as good as ours!), then I just wonder what His plan is for us, the sons of God! If God didn't want His servants sick, I don't believe He wants His sons to be sick.

I believe it is the plan of God that no believer should ever be sick. I believe every believer should live out his full length of time and, if Jesus tarries, actually wear out and then fall asleep in Him. It is not — and I state boldly, *not* — the will of God that we should suffer with cancer and other dreaded diseases which bring pain and anguish. No! It is God's will that we be healed. How do I know? Because healing is provided for us under the New Covenant.

✳

Memory Text:

"For I am not ashamed of the gospel of Christ: for it is the power of God unto salvation . . . ."

— Rom. 1:16

Healing:
God's Will for You

Bible Texts: John 10:10; Acts 10:38;
Luke 3:11-16; Exodus 23:25

Central Truth: Because God's Word declares
that healing is in God's plan of redemption,
you can know and be assured that
healing is God's will for you!

In church meetings, I'm sure many of us have seen marvelous healings and miracles occur as the Spirit of God manifested Himself through the gifts of the Spirit. But I believe we sometimes think the only way God heals is through manifestations of the gifts of the Spirit.

According to First Corinthians 12:7-10, gifts of healings and the working of miracles are manifestations of the Spirit of God. However, we can't always guarantee that God is going to move spectacularly through the gifts of the Spirit, because the Bible says, *"But all these [gifts] worketh that one and the selfsame Spirit, dividing to every man severally AS HE WILL"* (v. 11). Therefore, we do not always know when God will move spectacularly through the gifts of the Spirit.

However, we do know that God's Word *always* works.

The Word Works

We need to keep in mind that when the gifts of the Spirit are not in manifestation, people can still be healed through faith in God's Word. Therefore, we can always teach people the Word of God. In fact, I've seen just as many marvelous healings and miracles occur as a result of teaching people the Word of God, as I have when God moved miraculously through the gifts of the Spirit.

Healings and miracles can occur simply by teaching people the Word of God and by getting them to exercise their own faith for healing. You see, *the Word* is anointed. God's Word is the same whether I *feel* the anointing or not, and the Word always works!

Many times I think people are waiting for a manifestation of the Spirit of God to heal them. But they don't have to wait for a manifestation of the Spirit because the Word of God will always work for them!

For example, if doctors told you that you were going to die, would you just wait for a manifestation of the Spirit of God before you accepted the healing Jesus already provided for you? No, of course not!

Thank God, the Bible says, ". . . *Himself* [Jesus] *took our infirmities, and bare our sicknesses*" and ". . . *by whose stripes ye were healed*" (Matt. 8:17; 1 Peter 2:24)! If you *were healed* by Jesus' stripes, then you *are healed* now by His stripes.

I've seen more people healed in my ministry because they heard the Word and acted on their own faith, than any other way. Praise God, the Word works! That's the reason Paul told Timothy, "*Preach the word . . .*" (2 Tim. 4:2). Also, it's through *the Word* that we can be assured that it is God's will to heal us.

Satan Is the Author of Sickness

We know that it's God's will to heal His people because healing is in God's redemptive plan. We already read the scripture, ". . . *Himself took our infirmities, and bare our sicknesses*" (Matt. 8:17). So we know that healing is in the redemption that Jesus provided for us.

We also know that it's God's will to heal His people because sickness and disease come from Satan, and God does not want us to have anything that comes from Satan. We really don't have any business with something that doesn't belong to us. Sickness and disease don't belong to us — they're of the devil. By the same token, healing *does* belong to us. Jesus purchased healing for us in the plan of redemption through His death, burial, and resurrection.

Unless our minds are renewed with the Word of God, we won't understand that Satan is the author of sickness, disease, and everything that destroys. Our thinking will be all wrong. But once our minds are renewed with the Word of God, we will be able to see that Jesus came to redeem us from Satan's power and to give us life more abundantly.

JOHN 10:10
10 The thief [devil] cometh not, but for to steal, and to kill, and to destroy: I am come that they might have life, and that they might have it more abundantly.

Jesus' Earthly Ministry

According to John 10:10, anything which kills or destroys is from the enemy. The Bible also plainly tells us that when Satan is finally eliminated from the earth, the law of sin and death will stop functioning: there will be nothing that will hurt or destroy (Isa. 65:25).

Jesus came to do the will of God and to set men free, not to hurt or destroy lives. Therefore, it doesn't make sense to say that *God* hurts or destroys people's lives.

Jesus healed people in His earthly ministry, taking sickness *from* people, not putting sickness *on* them. That makes it impossible to accept the teaching that sickness and disease come from God. Jesus plainly taught by His words and His actions that sickness and disease come from the enemy, Satan.

ACTS 10:38

38 How God anointed Jesus of Nazareth with the Holy Ghost and with power: who went about doing good, and healing all that were oppressed of the devil; for God was with him.

Be Loosed From Satan's Bondages

LUKE 13:11-16

11 And, behold, there was a woman which had a spirit of infirmity eighteen years, and was bowed together, and could in no wise lift up herself.

12 And when Jesus saw her, he called her to him, and said unto her, Woman, thou art loosed from thine infirmity.

13 And he laid his hands on her: and immediately she was made straight, and glorified God.

14 And the ruler of the synagogue answered with indignation, because that Jesus had healed on the sabbath day, and said unto the people, There are six days in which men ought to work: in them therefore come and be healed, and not on the sabbath day.

15 The Lord then answered him, and said, Thou hypocrite, doth not each one of you on the sabbath loose his ox or his ass from the stall, and lead him away to watering?

16 And ought not this woman, being a daughter of Abraham, whom Satan hath bound, lo, these eighteen years, be loosed from this bond on the sabbath day?

Verse 11 says this woman had a spirit of infirmity. Where did the spirit of infirmity come from? Notice the phrase in verse 16: ". . .*whom SATAN HATH BOUND* . . . ." In verse 16 Jesus also declared that this woman should *be loosed* from this infirmity and gave two good reasons why.

One reason was that Satan had bound her. We know that sickness and disease are bondages. God's people should not be bound by sickness or disease because Jesus already paid the price for our redemption in the New Covenant.

The second reason Jesus said the woman should be healed was that she was a daughter of Abraham. I've heard people say, "Yes, but that's Old Covenant." However, we're under the New Covenant, and it's a *better* covenant established upon *better* promises. Certainly, if God's people can be healed under the Old Covenant, we can be healed under a new and better covenant!

To say that we have to be bound by Satan is wrong thinking! Galatians 3:29 says, ". . . *if ye be Christ's, then are ye Abraham's seed, and heirs according to the promise.*" And Galatians 3:7 says, "*Know ye therefore that they which are of faith, the same are the children of Abraham.*"

The woman in Luke 13 with the spirit of infirmity was a daughter or child of Abraham, and so are we — if we are in Christ! Jesus said this woman ought to be loosed. Well, if she ought to be loosed, then *we* ought to be loosed! Therefore, if Satan tries to bind us with sickness or disease, we don't have to accept that! We can be healed.

The Issue Is Settled

God calls sickness and disease satanic oppression. But, thank God, we read in Acts 10:38 that Jesus went about doing good in His earthly ministry, *healing all who were oppressed by the devil!* So many times people get confused and think God is the one who puts sickness and disease on them. But Acts 10:38 plainly states that Satan is the oppressor and that Jesus is the Deliverer! Let the Word of God — not man's ideas or opinions — settle this issue once and for all. *Healing is the will of God for you!*

EXODUS 23:25

25 And ye shall serve the Lord your God, and he shall bless thy bread, and thy water; and I will take sickness away from the midst of thee.

God told the children of Israel in Deuteronomy 28:15, ". . . *it shall come to pass, if thou wilt not hearken unto the voice of the Lord thy God, to observe to do all his commandments and his statutes which I command thee this day; that all these curses shall come upon thee, and overtake thee.*"

This verse doesn't mean that if the children of Israel disobeyed God, God would send curses upon them. It simply states that if they disobeyed God, the curses would *be able to* come upon them, because disobedience takes God's people out from under His protection!

By way of illustration, if you saw your child about to put his hand on a hot stove, you'd warn him, "Honey, don't do that! You'll get burned!" But if your child disobeyed you, and he put his hand on the stove anyway and burned himself, that wouldn't mean you *commissioned* or *authorized* that. Indirectly you permitted him to choose whether or not he would obey you, but you warned him what would happen if he did touch the hot stove.

Well, it's the same way with God. And it's only in that sense that God permits certain things to happen in our lives, because He has already warned us in His Word about the consequences of disobedience. He said in essence, "If you walk in My statutes and keep My commandments, *then* I'll take sickness away from the midst of you, and the number of your days I will fulfill" (Exod. 23:25,26).

I've also heard people say, "I was sick and I learned a great lesson from it." Well, I'm sure that any child who has ever burned his hand on a hot stove learned a lesson too. He learned not to put his hand on a hot stove! But that wasn't the way his parents would have chosen to teach him. And sickness and disease are not God's way of teaching us either. That would be cruel and God is not cruel.

The Word of God should settle the issue of God's willingness to heal you. Say it out loud: "Satan is the oppressor. Jesus is the Deliverer. With Jesus' stripes I am healed."

Jesus came that you might have life and have it more abundantly (John 10:10). Because God's Word declares that healing is in God's plan of redemption and that sickness and disease come from Satan, *not* God, you can know and be assured that healing is God's will for you!

Memory Text:
"And if ye be Christ's, then are ye Abraham's seed, and heirs according to the promise."
— Gal. 3:29

Two Streams Of Healing

Bible Texts: James 5:14-16;
Mark 5:25-30,34; Acts 10:38

Central Truth: The effectual, fervent prayer of the righteous causes God's healing power to be manifested. Our faith activates the anointing!

I've noticed that in the church world, people tend to treat important subjects like faith and prayer in a very general way. I think the same thing has happened with the subject of healing. Many times people just put all the scriptures on healing in the same sack, shake it up, and pour them all out together. It's no wonder that folks have become confused.

We need to learn to rightly divide the Word of God on every subject. For example, when we look at prayer, it's important to recognize there are different *kinds* of prayers. One kind of praying won't work where another kind of praying should, so it's necessary to find out what kind of prayer will work in each situation.

Well, when you study the subject of healing, you'll begin to see that

there are two streams or methods of healing found in the Scripture.

JAMES 5:14-16
14 Is any sick among you? let him call for the elders of the church; and let them pray over him, anointing him with oil in the name of the Lord:
15 And the prayer of faith shall save the sick, and the Lord shall raise him up; and if he have committed sins, they shall be forgiven him.
16 Confess your faults one to another, and pray one for another that ye may be healed. The effectual fervent prayer of a righteous man availeth much.

MARK 5:25-30,34
25 And a certain woman, which had an issue of blood twelve years,
26 And had suffered many things of many physicians, and had spent all

that she had, and was nothing bettered, but rather grew worse,

27 When she had heard of Jesus, came in the press behind, and touched his garment.

28 For she said, If I may touch but his clothes, I shall be whole.

29 And straightway the fountain of her blood was dried up; and she felt in her body that she was healed of that plague.

30 And Jesus, immediately knowing in himself that virtue [power, anointing] had gone out of him, turned him about in the press. . . .

34 And he said unto her, Daughter, thy faith hath made thee whole; go in peace, and be whole of thy plague.

In these scriptures we see these two streams of healing: one is *prayer* and the other is *being ministered to under the anointing.* Both will bring you the same results, but you need to understand that there's a difference between the two.

The Stream of Prayer

We know it's thoroughly scriptural to pray for the sick. Mark 11:24 says, ". . . *What things soever ye desire, when ye PRAY, believe that ye receive them, and ye shall have them.*" That would include healing, wouldn't it? Otherwise the scripture would have said, "What things soever you desire *except* healing . . . ." No, Mark 11:23 and 24 includes all things — *whatsoever* you desire

when you pray — as long as they're in line with God's Word!

These same two verses of Scripture brought me off the bed of sickness as a teenage boy. I had been bedfast for sixteen months with a deformed heart and an incurable blood disease. Five different medical doctors said I had to die because medical science couldn't do anything for me.

But something inside of me, the inward witness, said, "You don't have to die at this early age. You can be healed."

I began to meditate on Mark 11:23 and 24, because something inside of me told me I would find the answer for my healing there.

Now God may use some other passage of Scripture to lead you. You can't just lay some pattern down and say that's the way it's going to work with everybody. But with me, He used Mark 11:23 and 24. When I acted upon those verses, believing I received my healing when I prayed, I was healed!

The Prayer of Faith

You can be healed through prayer. In my case, I prayed the prayer of faith for myself. And you could do the same thing, because prayer is one stream of healing that's available to all of us!

On the other hand, you may not be in a position to pray. Your faith may not be at that level, or perhaps you haven't been taught along those lines. Then the Scripture also says, "*Is any sick among you? let him CALL FOR THE ELDERS of the church; and LET THEM PRAY over him. . . . And THE PRAYER OF FAITH SHALL SAVE THE SICK, and the Lord shall raise him up . . .*" (James 5:14,15).

I want to point out two or three things here that will be a blessing to you. First of all, the very fact that James asks the question, "Is any sick among you?" implies that there should not have been any sick among them.

Secondly, it proves that healing is for everyone. He didn't say, "Let them call for the elders of the church, and those whom it's God's will to heal will be healed, and those whom it's *not* God's will to be healed won't be healed." No, he said, "Is *any* sick among you?" So then, healing must be for "any" who are sick among us.

Then we also see that it's the prayer of faith that saves the sick. The same Greek word "sozo" translated *save* here is also translated *heal*. In other words, you could read it: "The prayer of faith shall *heal* the sick, and the Lord shall raise him up."

A person can pray in faith and receive healing for himself — the same way I did as a young boy when I was raised up from the bed of

sickness by faith in Mark 11:23 and 24. A person can also call for the elders of the church and let them pray over him — and the prayer of faith shall save the sick (James 5:14,15)!

James 5:16 goes on to say that believers can pray for one another that they might be healed, because ". . . The earnest (heartfelt, continued) prayer of a righteous man makes tremendous power available [dynamic in its working]" (*Amp.*)!

As Christians, we need to get this revelation down on the inside of us. The Bible says our effectual, fervent prayers can cause God's healing power to be manifested!

The Stream of the Anointing

The other method or stream of healing mentioned is *being ministered to with a tangible anointing* (Mark 5:30). In other words, you don't have to pray for God's healing power because it's already present to minister to people.

This is the stream of healing power that Jesus flowed in here on earth. Jesus never had to specifically *pray* for the sick because He was already *anointed* to *minister* healing to them (Acts 10:38).

Don't misunderstand. It's thoroughly scriptural to pray for the sick, and the Scriptures instruct you to do so. But, you see, there was no need for

Jesus to pray for something He already had — the healing anointing!

Jesus said in John 14:12: " . . . *He that believeth on me, the works that I do shall he do also; and greater works than these shall he do . . . . "*

Well, if we're going to do the works of Jesus in any measure, then it has to be with the same anointing. Therefore, we should learn something about how the anointing works.

Jesus used many methods of ministering healing, but the most prominent one seems to be the laying on of hands. You might say it was a point of contact through which the anointing could be transferred.

Also in connection with the laying on of hands, the Bible mentions two different times when people touched Jesus' clothes and they were healed (Matt. 14:35,36: Mark 5:30).

As we saw earlier in Mark 5:30, when the woman with the issue of blood touched Jesus' garment, " . . . *Jesus, immediately knowing in himself that VIRTUE had gone out of him, turned him about in the press, and said, Who touched my clothes?"*

The Greek word "virtue" is translated *power* throughout the *King James Version*. What was the power that went out of Jesus? It was healing power. It was the power with which He was anointed.

ACTS 10:38
38 How God anointed Jesus of Nazareth with the Holy Ghost and with power: who went about doing good, and healing all that were oppressed of the devil; for God was with him.

We know that Jesus works the same today because Hebrews 13:8 says that Jesus is the same yesterday, today, and forever. So if in His physical body Jesus was anointed with the Holy Ghost to heal and do good *yesterday*, then He's doing the same thing *today* through His Body, the Church. Therefore, He is *still* healing people by the anointing or power of the Holy Spirit!

Where did Jesus' power come from? God anointed Him with it!

Someone said, "But Jesus is the Son of God. He was God manifested in the flesh!" Yes, but the Word of God tells us that when Jesus came into this world, He laid aside the use of His mighty power and glory (Phil. 2:6-8). *The Amplified Bible* says that He " . . . stripped Himself [of all privileges and rightful dignity], so as to assume the guise of a servant (slave), in that He became like men and was born a human being" (v. 7).

Think about that for a moment. At age twenty-one, Jesus didn't heal anybody or work any miracles, yet He was just as much the Son of God then as He was when He was thirty years old. But the Word tells us that the Son of God *laid aside* the use of His mighty power and glory.

It was only after the Holy Ghost descended upon Jesus and He was *anointed* that He began to minister in the power of the Spirit (Luke 4:1-14). No miracles of healing took place until He was *anointed*.

So you see, it's the anointing of the Holy Spirit that brings the power! And this stream or method of healing — healing ministered by the anointing or power of the Holy Spirit — is still available today.

Faith Gives Action to the Power

Now there's something you need to understand about this stream through which the healing anointing is ministered: There is a role that *you* play as a receiver!

You see, even though God has anointed people to minister healing to the sick, folks must understand that healing is by degree. Therefore, it is based upon two conditions: the degree of healing power administered and the degree of a person's faith to receive.

When healing is ministered with a tangible anointing, the power of God is present to heal, but the person has a part to play too. It's the person's faith that gives action to the healing power of God that's transmitted to him.

Remember Jesus said to the woman with the issue of blood: *". . . Daughter, THY FAITH hath made thee whole . . ."* (Mark 5:34)! Somebody said, "I thought it was the anointing that healed her." Well, yes, it was, but it was the woman's faith that gave the healing anointing *action*.

Thank God, there are several methods of healing available to us because God desires for us to be whole and well. Prayer and the ministering of the tangible healing anointing are two of them. And with proper understanding, we can learn to flow with the Spirit of God in these two streams. Then we can use our faith to give *action* to God's healing power in our lives. But the main thing God wants us to know is that He wants us well and free!

Memory Text:
"And the prayer of faith shall save the sick, and the Lord shall raise him up . . . ."
— James 5:15

You Can Receive
If You Believe

Bible Texts: Mark 11:23,24; Matthew 21:22

Central Truth: Believing for the New Birth and being made a new creature is the biggest miracle there is. If you've already believed for that, you can believe for healing!

In my many years of ministering healing, I've discovered that the number one hindrance to receiving healing — you could call it the number one *enemy* to healing — is not knowing that it *is* God's will to heal. This is usually the issue you have to deal with in order for people to be healed. You have to get them to see that it is God's will to heal them!

I've also found that there is one group of people who do not believe that healing is for us today at all. In fact, they're sure it is *not* God's will to heal.

Then there is another group of people who believe in healing, all right — but they are certain that God won't heal *them*! They think they've been too evil, mean, or unworthy. (The devil will always bring up something.)

But we must not be found in either of these classes. We must get in the "Bible class" and find out what the Word of God teaches about divine healing.

My wife and I pastored for about twelve years, and during those years we never buried a church member. I just kept working with them until they were healed! I found out from experience how to help people receive their healing. Of course, sometimes it took me six months to help some people receive their healing, but eventually they were healed.

As I said, the main obstacle is getting people to believe that it is God's will to heal — that He *wants* to heal — and that they should be healed because it is His will.

Believe You Receive
When You Pray

Let me share with you a scriptural reason why it is God's will to heal you: *He promised to grant the things you ask for in believing prayer.* Let's examine what Jesus said about this subject in Mark 11.

MARK 11:23,24
23 For verily I say unto you, That whosoever shall say unto this mountain, Be thou removed, and be thou cast into the sea; and shall not doubt in his heart, but shall believe that those things which he saith shall come to pass; he shall have whatsoever he saith.
24 Therefore I say unto you, What things soever ye desire, when ye pray....

Notice verse 24 particularly. Jesus is talking about prayer here.

People who do not accept the Bible say, "Mark 11:24 isn't for everyone." In fact, I once heard a minister say, "Well, now, Mark 11:24 won't work for everyone."

I always respond to this argument with the question: "Is *prayer* for everyone? Or is it that some are supposed to pray and others are not?" You see, the subject in Mark 11 is *prayer*, it's not simply gaining the desire of your heart. Jesus tells you how to get "what things soever ye desire" through *prayer*, doesn't He?

How many should pray, then? Everyone. Well, if everyone should pray, then this verse belongs to everyone — because prayer belongs to everyone, doesn't it?

Let's look at verse 24 again: "*Therefore I say unto you, What things soever ye desire, when ye pray, believe that ye receive them, and ye shall have them.*" The *King James Version* says, "when you pray, believe that you receive *them*, and you shall have *them*." This is talking about the things you desire.

For now, we'll just consider one desire — healing for your body — and insert it into this verse. Now it reads, "When you pray, believe that you receive healing."

"But there's no physical change yet," some will argue.

I know it. Jesus said, "And *then* you'll have it." *But first you must believe you receive healing!*

"But I'm not healed!"

People who say this have already missed it, bless their hearts. They're going by their *heads* instead of their *hearts*.

When you pray, you have to *believe* that you *receive* healing, and *then* you will *have* healing. *When* are you going to have healing? *After* you *believe* you receive it. When do you *believe* you receive healing? *Before* you have it!

"But that doesn't make sense," someone will complain. "That's not even common sense."

I know. It's way above common sense. Did you ever read Isaiah chapter 55, where God said, *"For as the heavens are higher than the earth, so are my ways higher than your ways, and my thoughts than your thoughts"* (v. 9)? This kind of thinking is as high above common sense as the heavens are above the earth!

If you're a faith person (if you walk by faith) and someone is critical of you, don't feel embarrassed. The problem is that they can't see what you see, because God's Word is so far above their sight.

"That faith business! I don't believe in that!" People who say this are confessing that they're not saved, because the Bible says, *"For by grace are ye saved through FAITH . . ."* (Eph. 2:8). Doesn't it say that? Certainly, it does.

When you pray, *believe* that you *receive* healing and you will *have* healing. That's the revelation I received years ago as I lay bedfast and almost totally paralyzed on the bed of sickness. But I discovered that Mark 11:24 belongs to me! I still have the Bible I owned during that time, and you can see where I wrote

in red ink beside that verse, "This means me!"

'All' Includes Healing

Now the Bible states that in the mouth of two or three witnesses every word shall be established, so let's turn to Matthew 21 and see what Jesus said about believing:

MATTHEW 21:22
22 And all things, whatsoever ye shall ask in prayer, believing, ye shall receive.

How many things will you receive? All things but one? All things but healing? No, *all things*. If this promise did not include healing, then it would read "all things but one."

What if Jesus had said, "And all things, whatsoever ye shall ask in prayer, ye shall receive?" Then we'd automatically have it made, wouldn't we? Why did Jesus put that one little word — "believing" — in there? Because the promise won't work without it! Believing, believing, believing!

Believers Already Have Faith

Some say, "That's my trouble. I don't have any faith."

Why don't you get saved, then? *Saved people have faith.* That's who we are — saved people, believers.

Once during a crusade, a woman stopped me after a morning class and said, "Brother Hagin, I want you to pray for me."

I asked, "What for?"

She said, "I'm seventy-two years old, and I have high blood pressure and a severe heart condition. In fact, the doctors have just given up on me. They say I can't live much longer."

"Well, what do you want me to pray about?" I asked.

"I want you to pray that I'll have faith to be healed."

I said flatly, to get her attention, "Well, I'm not going to do it!"

It worked. She said, "You're not?"

"No, ma'am, I'm not."

"You're really not?"

"No, ma'am. I'm really not."

"Well!"

I saw I had gotten her attention, so I asked, "Aren't you a believer? Aren't you a child of God? Aren't you saved?"

"Oh, yes, yes! I'm a believer."

"Well," I said, "whoever heard of a believer who didn't believe? You've already believed for the biggest miracle there is. Believing for the New Birth and being made a new creature is the biggest miracle there is. If you've already believed for that, you can't believe for anything bigger than that!"

I continued, "Now suppose you had a grandson away at college, and you wrote him a letter every once in a while. Would you always add the postscript, 'Be sure not to forget to breathe'? No, you wouldn't remind him to breathe, because if he's already breathing, he's going to continue — and if he's not, all of your reminding won't help him!"

I explained, "You see, you are a believer — that's who you are. And all things whatsoever you ask in prayer *believing*, you shall receive. I lay hands on people because I believe."

She responded, "I'll be in the healing line tonight." And she was.

When I got to her, I said, "Well, I see you've come."

"Yes," she said, "and I'll be healed too! You just lay your hands on me." (You can see how she had changed since our conversation that morning.)

I laid my hand on her head and ministered healing to her, but I perceived that she didn't have the baptism of the Holy Spirit. (She was born again — born of the Spirit — but being filled with the Spirit is a different thing.)

I said, "You don't have the Holy Ghost."

She understood what I meant. "No," she said.

So I laid my hands on her head again and said, "Be filled with the Holy Ghost!" And instantly, without stammering or stuttering, she lifted both hands and began speaking in tongues fluently.

The point I'm making is, this woman already was a believer because she was born again. And once you're a born-again believer, all the promises in the Bible belong to you. This woman wanted me to pray that she would have faith to receive from God. But she had His promises all the time. She just didn't realize it.

There's an interesting sequel to this woman's story. Twenty-three years later, my wife and I were preaching in a nearby state, and after one of the night services, my wife asked me, "Wasn't that Sister So-and-so [this woman's daughter] in the service tonight?"

"Yes, it was" I said.

She had left the church before my wife was able to talk with her that night, but she was there the next morning, and Oretha and I were able to visit with her. We wondered if her mother was still alive. She was seventy-two years old when I prayed for her healing, and if she was still alive, that meant she would be ninety-five.

We asked, "Is your mother still alive?"

"Oh, yes."

"How is she?"

"She's in the best of health. Do you know, Brother and Sister Hagin, she's ninety-five now, and she only recently quit driving her car at night!"

I'm glad we didn't let her die at seventy-two when the doctors gave her up to die! Here she was at ninety-five, "still kicking," glory to God, and driving her own automobile! Why? Because she found out that when you pray, "all things" include healing: *All things* whatsoever you ask in prayer, *believing*, you shall receive. And that's who she was — a believer. So she could receive!

Say this out loud: "I'm a believer." Well, it shouldn't be hard for you to *believe*, then, should it?

✳

Memory Text:

"Therefore I say unto you, What things soever ye desire, when ye pray, believe that ye receive them, and ye shall have them."

— Mark 11:24

Healing Is a Good Gift

Bible Texts: James 5:13-16; John 14:16,17; Matthew 7:11; James 1:17

Central Truth: The Word of God tells us that Jesus went about doing good and healing all that were oppressed of the devil — that means healing is good!

A key verse in the study of why it's God's will to heal is a familiar one found in Acts 10:38: *"How God anointed Jesus of Nazareth with the Holy Ghost and with power: who went about DOING GOOD, AND HEALING all that were oppressed of the devil; for God was with him."*

Some people say, "I don't know whether it's the will of God to heal me or not."

Jesus said, *". . . I came down from heaven, not to do mine own will, but the will of him that sent me"* (John 6:38). What did Jesus do here on earth? We read in Acts 10:38 that He went about *doing good and healing.* Since that is so, then doing good and healing *have* to be the will of God, don't they?

People sometimes get confused about the character of God because

they believe something other than what the Bible says about Him. *But if you want to see God in action, look at Jesus!* Jesus said, *". . . he that hath seen me hath seen the Father . . ."* (John 14:9).

Always remember that Jesus' actions reflected the will of God in action. And what did Jesus do? He went about *doing good and healing* all that were oppressed of the devil, for God was with Him. That means healing is *good,* doesn't it?

This can be summed up in the text, Matthew 7:11: *"If ye then, being evil, know how to give GOOD gifts* [we found out that healing is *good*] *unto your children, HOW MUCH MORE shall your Father which is in heaven give good things to them that ask him?"*

No Quick Fixes

Before studying something else in Matthew, let's look at three questions James asks:

JAMES 5:13-15
13 Is any among you afflicted? let him pray. Is any merry? let him sing psalms.
14 Is any sick among you? let him call for the elders of the church; and let them pray over him, anointing him with oil in the name of the Lord:
15 And the prayer of faith shall save the sick, and the Lord shall raise him up; and if he have committed sins, they shall be forgiven him.

Notice that James is talking about three different things here: Is any *afflicted*? Is any *merry*? Is any *sick*?

The Greek word translated "afflicted" means *to go through a test or trial or to be depressed or oppressed*. The word "afflicted" does not mean sick. Also notice that the individual who is afflicted is to do his own praying! So James is really saying, "Is anyone being tested? Is anyone going through a trial? Let him pray." Notice it doesn't say, "Let him get someone to pray for him." No, James said, "Let *him* pray." (Another person could never be as concerned about your problems as you are.)

People today are looking for a "quick fix." But God doesn't have any "quick fixes"! He's not putting on any 99-cent sales. And He doesn't have blessings priced two for a quarter. I don't mean to be funny about this, but it's absolutely the truth. That's the reason James asked, "Is any among you afflicted? Let *him* pray!" (Him who? The one who's afflicted — and that means "her" too.) Then James adds, "Is any merry? Let *him* sing."

Isn't it strange that when someone is afflicted, that person usually wants you to do the praying for him. However, when he's merry, he doesn't want you to sing for him — he wants to do the singing *himself*!

Many times people are looking for someone else to tell them what to do. But you can't be responsible for other people, and you can't tell them what to do.

If a person will just listen to the Bible, he'll *know* what to do. "What if he doesn't know what the Bible says?" you may ask. Then if he'll get alone with God, the Holy Spirit will speak to his spirit!

The Bible says, *"The spirit of man in the candle of the Lord, searching all the inward parts of the belly"* (Prov. 20:27). In other words, God will direct you through your spirit.

I know from experience that this works. People have come to me for advice, and I've said, "Well, let's pray." And we got down on our knees and prayed for as much as an hour. Afterwards, when I asked them what their problem was, they replied, "Oh, I already have the answer, bless God. I got it while we were praying." I never did have to counsel them.

Our Counselor

JOHN 14:16,17
16 And I [Jesus] **will pray the Father, and he shall give you another Comforter, that he may abide with you for ever;**
17 Even the Spirit of truth. . . .

The Greek word translated "Comforter" in verse 16 is *paraclete,* a word that has a sevenfold meaning: Comforter, Helper, Counselor, Advocate, Intercessor, Strengthener, and Standby. What more would you need?

That's why James said, "Is any afflicted? Is any going through a test? Is any in trouble? Let him pray?" Why? *Because when you're in prayer, the Holy Spirit, who is your built-in Counselor, will give you direction!*

Have you ever noticed how many times the Holy Spirit will take the Word and open it up to you while you're praying? Jesus promised His disciples that the Holy Spirit would bring His words to the remembrance of those who believe in Him.

Whatever God said in His Word, He said to us. It belongs to us. And the Holy Spirit will bring God's words to our attention while we're praying. But He can't bring them to our attention if we ignore Him and run to other people for help!

Don't misunderstand me — others ought to help us if they can. But if we do what the Bible says, it will solve our problems. We will get *permanent* help.

Well, what does the Bible say? "Is any among you afflicted? Let him pray."

Do you need comfort? There's a *Comforter* on the inside of you — the Holy Spirit. Do you need help? The *Helper* is inside you. Do you need counsel? The *Counselor* is inside you. Do you need an advocate — one who pleads your case? The Holy Spirit is your *Advocate.* Do you need an intercessor? He'll help you intercede. Do you need strength and someone to stand by you? He's your *Strengthener.* He's your *Standby.* That means He's just standing by in case you need Him. He's there.

Now let's look at something else in James.

JAMES 5:14-16
14 Is any sick among you? let him call for the elders of the church; and let them pray over him, anointing him with oil in the name of the Lord:

**15 And the prayer of faith shall save the sick, and the Lord shall raise him up; and if he have committed sins, they shall be forgiven him.
16 Confess your faults one to another, and pray one for another, that ye may be healed. The effectual fervent prayer of a righteous man availeth much.**

Many years ago, the leading Greek scholar in the United States told me that verse 14 in the original Greek literally says, "Are any beyond doing anything for themselves? Let them call for the elders of the church."

There are many directions we could go here, but the point I'm making is based on verse 16: "... *pray one for another, that ye may be healed ... .* " Healing must be a good thing, because God wouldn't tell us to pray for something that wasn't good, would He? And if it's good, then healing must be the will of God — especially for Christians.

Would God tell you to pray for something that wasn't His will? That would be stupid, wouldn't it? And I don't believe God is stupid!

What Is a Good Gift?

MATTHEW 7:11

11 If ye then, being evil, know how to give good gifts unto your children, how much more [some of you need to say that to yourselves until you start shouting about "how much more"] **shall your Father which is in heaven give good things to them that ask him?**

From the standpoint of the Fatherhood of God, Matthew 7:11 says that He'll give good things to us. But He told us to ask for them. And He said, "Pray one for another." So healing belongs to us. Say this out loud: "Healing belongs to me. God wants me well!"

Our Heavenly Father gives good things to them that ask Him. Well, what is good? Acts 10:38 tells us that Jesus went about doing good — and healing. Healing is good!

I want to ask you another question, since we're talking about healing: *Is sickness a good thing?* If it is, we ought to never want to get rid of it. We ought to want to keep it. But it's not a good thing to be sick and off work, to lose your job, to see your children go hungry, and to lose your automobile and home. (You could ask just anybody on the street about that, and they would know better!)

Likewise, *Is healing a good thing?* Well, if you're hurting, doesn't it feel good when the hurting stops? Yes, it is a good thing to be well and healthy, to be able to stay on the job, and to provide for your family. Anyone would know that's good, even from the natural standpoint.

Let's see what else the Bible says.

JAMES 1:17

17 Every good gift and every perfect gift is from above, and cometh down from the Father of lights, with whom is no variableness, neither shadow of turning.

The Heavenly Father never changes. He doesn't vary the least bit. And every good gift and every perfect gift is from above.

That means sickness and disease could not be *good* gifts, because sickness and disease don't come down from Heaven. It would be impossible — *because there's no sickness or disease up there!*

In what is commonly referred to as "The Lord's Prayer," the disciples are told to pray, "... *Thy will be done in earth, as it is in heaven*" (Matt. 6:10). Now if it is the will of God for His children to be sick on earth, then it has to be His will for them to be sick in Heaven. And we've already learned that they can't be sick in Heaven, because the Bible says there is no sickness there. If we are told to pray, "Thy will be done on earth, as it is in Heaven," then we are told to pray that there *not* be any sickness on earth. It is just that simple.

If sickness can't come from Heaven, then it could not be a good gift, according to the biblical definition. Yet I've actually heard ministers say, "Well, we don't know what's good for us — God does. And He sometimes puts sickness on people."

God certainly doesn't put sickness on people, because He doesn't have any! You can't give somebody something that you don't have. So if there's no sickness in Heaven, where would God get it in order to put it on you? He'd have to steal it from the devil, and God's not a thief!

Every *good* gift and every *perfect* gift is from *above*. This must mean the *healing comes from Heaven*, because Jesus came from Heaven, and He Himself took our infirmities and bore our sicknesses (Matt. 8:17)!

✳

Memory Text:

"Every good gift and every perfect gift is from above, and cometh down from the Father of lights ...."

— James 1:17

Is It God's Will
To Heal You?

Bible Texts: Isaiah 53:4,5;
Matthew 8:17; 1 Peter 2:24

Central Truth: The object of Jesus' sin-bearing
was that we might be free from sin,
and the object of His sickness-bearing
was that we might be free from sickness.

Scripture reveals the *nature* of God to us. It also reveals the *attitude* of God toward sin, sickness, and disease. God's nature has not changed through the ages. Neither has His attitude changed toward sin, sickness, and disease.

You need to know this in order to understand divine healing. In fact, the first principal fact you should know about divine healing is: *It is God's will to heal you, because healing is in His redemptive plan.*

The Bible says that in the mouth of two or three witnesses every word shall be established (Matt. 18:16). Notice that the following texts from Isaiah, Matthew, and First Peter all agree that Jesus took our infirmities and bore our sicknesses.

ISAIAH 53:4,5
4 **Surely he** [Jesus] **hath borne our griefs** [sicknesses]**, and carried our sorrows** [diseases]**: yet we did esteem him stricken, smitten of God, and afflicted.**
5 **But he was wounded for our transgressions, he was bruised for our iniquities: the chastisement of our peace was upon him; and with his stripes we are healed.**

This passage of Scripture is taken from the *King James Version*. A good reference Bible will have a marginal note by the words "griefs" and "sorrows" (v. 4) to tell you that the Hebrew words are literally "sicknesses" and "diseases." Dr. Isaac Leeser's translation of *The Hebrew Bible*, a translation authorized for use by Orthodox Jews, reads: "Our *diseases* did he bear himself, and our *pains* he carried: while we indeed esteemed him stricken, smitten of God, and afflicted."

MATTHEW 8:17

17 That it might be fulfilled which was spoken by Esaias the prophet, saying, Himself took our infirmities, and bare our sicknesses.

This text is clearer yet. Matthew is quoting Isaiah. If you check the reference, you'll find that he is quoting Isaiah 53:4. I like to say it this way: "Jesus took *my* infirmities and bare *my* sicknesses."

I read this verse for years before I understood what it was saying: Jesus actually — literally — took the cause of our sickness and disease. He took our infirmities and bare our sicknesses.

We know that Jesus was made to be sin for us (2 Cor. 5:21). The object of His sin-bearing was that we might be free from sin, and the object of His sickness-bearing was that we might be free from sickness. This truth is also reflected in First Peter 2:24:

1 PETER 2:24

24 Who his own self bare our sins in his own body on the tree, that we, being dead to sins, should live unto righteousness: by whose stripes ye were healed.

Thus, three witnesses — Isaiah, Matthew, and Peter — tell us not only that Jesus shed His blood for the remission of our sins but that with His stripes, we were healed. Some people do not believe this. I once read a commentary whose author said that "by whose stripes ye were healed" does not mean physical healing; it means spiritual healing. So according to the commentary, your *spirit* is healed by His stripes.

God, however, does not *heal* the spirit of the sinner. He recreates it and makes the person a new creature.

Jeremiah and Ezekiel, prophesying in the Old Testament, said, *"Behold, the days come, saith the Lord, that I will make a new covenant with the house of Israel ....";* "... *and I will put a new spirit within you; and I will take the stony heart out of their flesh, and will give them an heart of flesh"* (Jer. 31:31; Ezek. 11:19).

Those who believe that God heals man's spirit do not believe that man ever failed or sinned. Their unscriptural propaganda says that all of us have a spark of divinity that God needs to perfect. No! A sinner needs to be born again to become a new man — the new creature described in Second Corinthians 5:17: *"Therefore if any man be in Christ, he is a NEW CREATURE: old things are passed away; behold, all things are become new.*" (The marginal note here says that he is a *"new creation."*)

When a person gets *healed,* however, old things do not pass away and become new — just the sickness passes away. The part that was diseased becomes new. (If I have a boil on my nose and that boil gets healed, I don't get a new nose. It's the same nose I always had. Just the diseased part is gone.)

Therefore, First Peter 2:24 does not mean spiritual healing; it means just what it said. As I read further from this gentleman's commentary, I thought, *If this means spiritual healing, then the Lord Himself didn't know it and He made a mistake.* I was recalling an incident that happened during a meeting I held in Oklahoma.

One of the seven cooperating churches was pastored by a couple I had known in Texas. They said, "We're going to bring a woman from our church for prayer one night, Brother Hagin. She's crippled and hasn't walked a step in four years. We've taken her to the best specialists in the state, and they all say she'll never walk again 'the longest day she lives.'"

Ordinarily I minister under the anointing. But on the night she came, I had ministered to so many people that by the time I got to her, I was exhausted. (The Lord is the same all the time, but I am not.

Potentially, the anointing is present all the time, but in manifestation, it's not — and when you grow weary, it is difficult to yield to God.)

Since the anointing was no longer in manifestation by the time I got to this woman, I couldn't conscientiously minister to her as I normally would. Her pastors had brought her to the meeting from a distance, and what was I to do? Just send her away?

No, there was still a way to minister to her — because God's Word never fails! The *manifestation* of the anointing may wane, disappear, and be gone. But the Word of God is anointed forever, and His words are Spirit and Life! Hallelujah!

So I sat down on the altar beside the woman, opened my Bible to First Peter 2:24, laid the Bible on her lap, and asked her to read it.

Then I asked her, "Is the word 'were' past tense, future tense, or present tense?"

A look of recognition flashed across her face like a neon light lighting up in the dark. "Why," she said, "it's past tense. And if we *were* healed, I *was* healed!" (That is believing in line with God's Word.)

I said, "Sister, will you do what I tell you to do?"

"Well," she said, "I will if it's easy."

I said, "It's the easiest thing you ever did in your life. Just lift up your hands and start praising God, because you *are* healed — not *going to be* — *are!*"

I wish you could have seen that crippled woman. She had no evidence of healing. She had not yet walked a step. But she lifted her hands, looked up, and as a smile broke across her face, she said, "Oh, dear Father God — *whooo!* I'm so glad I'm healed! Oh, Lord, You know how tired I got sitting around these last few years. I'm so glad I'm not helpless and I don't need to be waited on anymore." (You see, she was acting on the Word. That's what faith is.)

I stood and told the congregation, "Let's all lift our hands and praise God with her, because she is healed." (And yet, from all observation, she was still sitting on the altar, crippled.)

After we stopped, I turned to the woman and said, "Now, my sister, rise and walk in Jesus' Name!"

God and hundreds of people are my eternal witnesses that she instantly leaped to her feet, and she jumped, ran, and danced — just like the lame man who went into the Temple, walking, leaping, and praising God (Acts 3:8).

We all shouted and cried with her. Then somebody went off and told a lie about me! He said, "That fellow, Hagin, healed a crippled woman last night."

But I didn't have any more to do with it than you or anybody else could have. *Jesus healed her nearly 2,000 years ago, and she just found out about it that night!*

The point I am making is that although that so-called minister said, "First Peter 2:24 doesn't mean physical healing," it was the only verse I gave the crippled woman! I thought to myself, *If that verse means only spiritual healing, then God made a mistake. He should have healed her spiritually, not physically!*

Friends, First Peter 2:24 means just what it says, and it belongs to us now. Bless God, by Jesus' stripes we *were* healed!

Our Rights To Be Healed

Jesus not only redeemed us from sin, He redeemed us from sickness. So it *is* God's will to heal you. Never doubt it, because healing is in His redemptive plan.

Not only is healing in God's *redemptive plan*, but because Jesus sealed the New Covenant with His own blood, we also have a *legal right* to divine healing (Heb. 8:6; 12:24; 13:20)!

The New Covenant guarantees us the rights and privileges that Jesus secured for us, which include divine healing. In Mark 11:24 He said, ". . . *What things soever ye desire, when ye pray, believe that ye receive them, and ye shall have them.*"

Therefore, we have a *prayerful right* to divine healing!

Then in Psalm 23, the Psalmist talks about Jesus as our Redeemer, saying, *"Thou PREPAREST A TABLE BEFORE ME in the presence of mine enemies. . . [v. 5]."* Therefore healing is our *provisional right* — our Heavenly Father has prepared a table of provision for us, and it includes healing!

Incline Your Ear

The Master is calling you to take your place at the banqueting table and dine! He invites you to partake of divine healing and every other privilege that belongs to you in Christ! How? By inclining your ear to God's Word, because God's Word is His will.

Since God's Word is His will, you could say, "The Bible is God personally speaking to me."

Someone said, "Yes, I know what the Bible says about healing. But I don't believe it just that way."

Well, if you have that attitude, you are not inclining your ear to God's sayings — to His Word. Instead, you are inclining your ear to your own beliefs and opinions.

Some Christians don't incline their ears unto God's sayings because they always want to hear something *new* from the Word. When someone preaches or teaches on the subjects of faith and healing, they say, "Oh, I've heard all that before." But those folks aren't inclining their ears to God's sayings!

You see, the Word doesn't work for you because you *have inclined* your ear once or twice to God's sayings. No, "incline your ear" is present tense. That means it's an ongoing, continual action.

Proverbs 4:20 and 22 says, *". . . INCLINE thine ear unto my sayings. . . . For they are life unto those that find them, and HEALTH* [medicine] *to all their flesh."* Why should you incline your ear unto the Word of God? Because God's Word is *medicine.* It's a never-failing remedy for all your flesh, which includes everything that pertains to your life.

Memory Text:
"Who his own self bare our sins in his own body on the tree, that we, being dead to sins, should live unto righteousness: by whose stripes ye were healed."
— 1 Peter 2:24

God's Word Is Health to Our Flesh!

Bible Texts: Proverbs 4:20-22; John 6:63;
Matthew 15:21-28; 8:1-3, 5-10, 13-17

Central Truth: God's words are full of life,
health, and healing, and they act
like medicine for all your flesh!

God wants us to understand the life and power that's in His Word. When God made the world, He created the earth, the sky, and the great expanse of this universe with *words*.

But God's *words* are a never-failing remedy for any situation or circumstance that might come your way in life, including sickness and disease. Proverbs 4:22 says God's words ". . . *are LIFE unto those that find them, and HEALTH to all their flesh.*"

PROVERBS 20:20-22
20 My son, attend to my words; incline thine ear unto my sayings.
21 Let them not depart from thine eyes; keep them in the midst of thine heart.
22 For they are life unto those that find them, and health to all their flesh.

JOHN 6:63
63 . . . the words that I [Jesus] speak unto you, they are spirit, and they are life.

God's words are full of life, health, and healing, and they act like medicine. In fact, the margin of my Bible reads, "My words are medicine." Medicine for what? *For all your flesh!*

Proverbs 4:20 says, ". . . *attend to my WORDS . . . .*" That means *give God's Word your undivided attention.* In other words, put God's Word *into your heart*, and put out of your heart everything that exalts itself against the Word.

The rest of verse 20 says, ". . . *incline thine ear unto my sayings.*" *That* means *take in God's Word through your ear gates or open your ears to God's sayings.* If you're attending to God's Word and *opening* your ears to His sayings, you're *closing* your ears to other sayings, such as fear, doubt, and unbelief.

We are to look at God's Word as well as listen to God's Word. Proverbs 4:21 says, *"Let them not depart from thine eyes . . . ."* This scripture doesn't mean we are to be continuously looking at the Word so that we never do anything else. It means we are to always look to the Word of God instead of at the circumstances. In the good times and in the bad, we are to just keep looking at God's words — at His sayings.

There's power in God's Word! There's healing in His Word too. Notice Proverbs 4:22 again: *"For they* [God's words] *are life unto those that find them, and health to all their flesh."* God's words are full of life, health, and healing!

The Children's Bread

The Word has a lot to say about divine healing. For instance, in Matthew 15:21-28 we read that healing is the children's bread.

MATTHEW 15:21-28
21 Then Jesus went thence, and departed into the coasts of Tyre and Sidon.
22 And, behold, a woman of Canaan came out of the same coasts, and cried unto him, saying, Have mercy on me, O Lord, thou son of David; my daughter is grievously vexed with a devil.
23 But he answered her not a word. And his disciples came and **besought him, saying, Send her away; for she crieth after us.**
24 But he answered and said, I am not sent but unto the lost sheep of the house of Israel.
25 Then came she and worshipped him, saying, Lord, help me.
26 But he answered and said, It is not meet to take the children's bread, and to cast it to dogs.
27 And she said, Truth, Lord: yet the dogs eat of the crumbs which fall from their master's table.
28 Then Jesus answered and said unto her, O woman, great is thy faith: be it unto thee even as thou wilt. And her daughter was made whole from that very hour.

Healing is the children's bread! These are Jesus' own words! You can incline your ear to the fact that healing is your bread, because Jesus said it. That means if you're born again, then you're God's child, and *healing belongs to you!* It would help you to say it out loud: "Healing belongs to me. It's my bread!"

Some of you need to incline your ear unto that and say it long enough for it to register on the inside of you, in your spirit. The Word won't work for you if it's just in your head. But when the Word gets on the inside of you — in your spirit — then results are forthcoming!

God's Medicine

Proverbs says, *". . . incline thine ear unto my sayings. . . . For they are life unto those that find them, and health* [medicine] *to all their flesh"* (vv. 20,22). Since God's Word is medicine to all our flesh, we need to know how to take God's medicine, His Word, and appropriate it for the healing of our bodies.

We take God's medicine by doing what Proverbs 4:20 and 21 says to do: (1) *Attend* to God's Word; (2) *incline* our ears unto it; (3) *let it not depart* from our eyes; (4) *keep* it in the midst of our heart. All these instructions imply a continual, ongoing action, not something we do one time or every once in a while.

In the natural, suppose you had an illness last year, and your doctor prescribed a certain kind of medicine for you to take. Then suppose you got sick again this year with the same illness, and the doctor prescribed the same kind of medicine for you. You wouldn't tell him, "Oh, no, Doctor! I can't take that medicine. I took some of that *last* year!"

Well, the dose you took *last year* isn't going to do you a bit of good if you need medicine again *this year.* It's the same way with God's Word. For example, God's Word won't benefit you if you have the attitude, *I've heard all that before.* No, in order for God's Word to do you any good, you have to stay with it. You have to keep taking God's medicine.

You see, the Bible says faith is the victory (1 John 5:4). And faith comes by hearing the Word of God, not by *having heard* it (Rom. 10:17)!

Great Faith

MATTHEW 8:5-10,13
5 And when Jesus was entered into Capernaum, there came unto him a centurion, beseeching him,
6 And saying, Lord, my servant lieth at home sick of the palsy, grievously tormented.
7 And Jesus saith unto him, I will come and heal him.
8 The centurion answered and said, Lord, I am not worthy that thou shouldest come under my roof: but speak the word only, and my servant shall be healed.
9 For I am a man under authority, having soldiers under me: and I say to this man, Go, and he goeth; and to another, Come, and he cometh; and to my servant, Do this, and he doeth it.
10 When Jesus heard it, he marvelled, and said to them that followed, Verily I say unto you, I have not found so great faith, no, not in Israel. . . .
13 And Jesus said unto the centurion, Go thy way; and as thou hast believed, so be it done unto thee. And his servant was healed in the selfsame hour.

Jesus called the centurion's faith *great faith*! What is great faith? The answer is found in verse 8. The centurion said to Jesus, *"Speak the word only,* and my servant will be healed." Great faith is simply faith in God's Word. It's taking God at His Word.

God wants us to have the same great faith that the centurion had. He wants us to have confidence in the authority of His Word. Because of the centurion's great faith, Jesus said unto him, "... *Go thy way; and as thou hast believed, so be it done unto thee ...* " (v. 13). I believe Jesus is saying to each of us today: "Go your way, and as you have believed, so be it done unto you."

The Bible says God never changes (Mal. 3:6; Heb. 13:8). What He has done for anyone else, He will do for you, if you will believe Him and take Him at His Word. God is no respecter of persons (Acts 10:34). He doesn't favor one person more than another. He favors anyone who is committed to believing His Word.

God's Willingness To Heal

MATTHEW 8:1-3

1 When he [Jesus] was come down from the mountain, great multitudes followed him.
2 And, behold, there came a leper and worshipped him, saying, Lord, if thou wilt, thou canst make me clean.
3 And Jesus put forth his hand, and touched him, saying, I will; be thou clean. And immediately his leprosy was cleansed.

MATTHEW 8:14-17

14 And when Jesus was come into Peter's house, he saw his wife's mother laid, and sick of a fever.
15 And he touched her hand, and the fever left her: and she arose, and ministered unto them.
16 When the even was come, they brought unto him many that were possessed with devils: and he cast out the spirits with his word, and healed all that were sick:
17 That it might be fulfilled which was spoken by Esaias the prophet, saying, Himself took our infirmities, and bare our sicknesses.

There are a lot of truths we could expound on in these verses. But I think one great truth that outshines the rest is God's willingness to heal everyone. Notice in the first passage that the leper believed Jesus *could* heal him, but he questioned whether or not Jesus *would* heal him. The leper said, "... *Lord, IF THOU WILT, thou canst make me clean*" (v. 2). Jesus settled the issue once and for all when He plainly answered the man, "I will" (v. 3). Yet many folks today follow the leper's *unbelief* about healing rather than Jesus' *willingness* to heal.

Now take a look at the second passage of Scripture from Matthew 8. In verses 14 and 15 we read that Jesus healed Peter's mother-in-law.

Many believe it is God's will to heal *some people* or a selected few, such as the mother-in-law of one of Jesus' disciples. But they don't believe it's God's will to heal everyone.

But notice that the same day Jesus healed Peter's mother-in-law, He also healed all those in need: "*When the even was come, they brought unto him MANY that were possessed with devils: and he cast out the spirits with his word, and healed ALL that were sick*" (v. 16).

Why did Jesus heal the multitudes? The very next verse says He healed them *"That it might be fulfilled which was spoken by Esaias the prophet, saying, Himself took our infirmities, and bare our sicknesses"* (v. 17). Jesus was moved by compassion to heal the sick (Matt. 9:36).

So we know from the Word that healing does not belong to just a selected few. God doesn't favor some but not others. For example, the Bible doesn't say, "Himself took *Peter's mother-in-law's* infirmities and bore *her* sicknesses"! And it doesn't say, "Himself took *the centurion's servant's* infirmities and bore his sicknesses"!

No, the Bible says, *". . . Himself took OUR infirmities, and bare OUR sicknesses"* (Matt. 8:17)! And it was on the basis of this truth that Jesus healed the multitudes. Jesus healed *"all* that were sick" who came to Him (v. 16).

I've been in the healing ministry for quite some time now, and I have found that the biggest difficulty to getting people healed is to convince them that it is God's *will* to heal. Many Christians make some effort to approach God and receive healing, yet many times the thought lurks in the back of their minds, *I know God does heal people, but it might not be His will to heal me.*

But, you see, these folks aren't inclining their ears unto God's sayings. When you incline your ear to what God says, you *know* the will of God concerning healing. And over and over again, God's willingness to heal is expressed in the pages of His Word.

Let's listen to God's Word continually and incline our ears unto *His* sayings. I've said many times that just because I ate one T-bone steak doesn't mean I'm never going to eat another one. In a similar sense, just as continually feeding your *body* with good food keeps it strong, continually feeding your spirit with God's Word keeps your *spirit* strong and your faith alive.

When you feed your spirit on God's Word along the lines of healing, you are building health and healing into your body, because God's Word is health to all your flesh!

The Abundant Life

Bible Texts: Acts 10:38; Hebrews 1:1,2; Matthew 7:7-11; John 10:10; Proverbs 4:20-22; Mark 11:24

Central Truth: If you'll get into the Word of God, the Holy Ghost will illuminate your mind and your spirit, and you will see that God is the Healer.

In the previous lesson we saw that we can know the will of God in the situations and circumstances of life by inclining our ears to God's sayings (Prov. 4:20)! God's *Word* is God's *will*.

There is peace and comfort in knowing the will of God. As the Psalmist of old said, *"How precious also are thy thoughts unto me, O God! how great is the sum of them!"* (Ps. 139:17).

We also said in a few earlier lessons that Jesus' earthly ministry was the will of God in action on the behalf of mankind. Jesus said in John 6:38, *". . . I came down from heaven, not to do mine own will, but the will of him that sent me."*

ACTS 10:38
38 How God anointed Jesus of Nazareth with the Holy Ghost and with power: who went about doing good, and healing all that were oppressed of the devil; for God was with him.

Was Jesus doing God's will when He went about doing good and healing all who were oppressed by the devil? Certainly, He was!

God Never Changes!

Has God's will changed about healing all those who are oppressed by the devil? Of course not, because the Bible says God never changes (Mal. 3:6; Heb. 13:8). So we can know for certain that it is God's will to heal everyone.

Acts 10:38 should be enough to convince us that it is God's will to heal today, but there are many other verses that also reveal to us God's

49

will concerning healing. That's why we should incline our ears to God's Word — to His sayings — because His words are life to those who find them and health to all their flesh (Prov. 4:22). God's Word is medicine!

I've said before that the Bible is God speaking to each one of us personally. And Jesus' earthly ministry was the express will of God in action. Since Jesus was God who came in the flesh (John 1:1,14), we could also say that *Jesus* is God speaking to us personally.

HEBREWS 1:1,2
1 God, who at sundry times and in divers manners spake in time past unto the fathers by the prophets,
2 Hath in these last days spoken unto us by his Son, whom he hath appointed heir of all things, by whom also he made the worlds.

If Jesus is God speaking to us, what is God saying? Is God saying it is not His will to heal or that it is His will to heal only a few? Certainly not. *God reveals in His Word that He never changes.* In other words, whatever He has done for anyone else, He will do for each of us, if we will take Him at His Word and trust Him.

Are You Limiting God?

In His Word God also reveals to us that He is a kind, loving Heavenly Father.

MATTHEW 7:7-11
7 Ask, and it shall be given you; seek, and ye shall find; knock, and it shall be opened unto you:
8 For every one that asketh receiveth; and he that seeketh findeth; and to him that knocketh it shall be opened.
9 Or what man is there of you, whom if his son ask bread, will he give him a stone?
10 Or if he ask a fish, will he give him a serpent?
11 If ye then, being evil, know how to give good gifts unto your children, how much more shall your Father which is in heaven give good things to them that ask him?

How much more will God give good things to us! This passage of Scripture is saying that as a natural father loves his children and desires the best for them, our Heavenly Father loves His children *much more* and desires to give us good things in life.

For instance, if your child was burning up with fever, how many of you parents would heal him if you could? Certainly you would make your child well if it were in your power to do so. Well, thank God, God wants to do the same for His children, and *God is able!*

Someone asked, "If God is able, then why doesn't He just heal every sick person?"

God is omnipotent or all-powerful. But He can only do in a person's life what that person allows Him to do.

Some will argue that since God is omnipotent, He can make people do anything He wants them to do. But if that were true, He'd make all sinners get saved, and He'd make all Christians pay their tithes!

No, God can't do any more in your life than you permit Him to do. Jesus said, *"Behold, I stand at the door, and knock: if any man* [will] *hear my voice, and open the door, I will come in to him, and will sup with him, and he with me"* (Rev. 3:20).

Man is a free moral agent — he has the ability and the right to make his own choices. He can choose to accept Jesus Christ as Savior and Lord and be born again, or he can reject Jesus.

Even after you are born again, you don't lose your will or right to choose. You have a choice as to what you will do with God's Word. Will you attend to it? Will you incline your ear to it? Will you keep it before your eyes and in the midst of your heart?

If you do, God's Word will become life and health to you. God's Word is a never-failing remedy for all your flesh and for all the problems of life that may try to come your way!

People bring a lot of trouble on themselves. And, of course, the devil accommodates them in wrongdoing too. People get into trouble when they don't do what the Bible says to do.

You can spare yourself a lot of misery in life by just doing what the Bible says — by inclining your ear to God's sayings!

Inclining Our Ears

You need to incline your ear to what God's Word says about every area of your life. When you obey one part of the Bible, it makes it a whole lot easier to obey other parts of the Bible.

On the other hand, if you disobey God's Word along one particular line, it makes it easier to disobey God's Word in other areas. And when you're in disobedience, it opens the door for the devil to try to work in your life. It's just better to listen and pay attention to what the Bible says.

We need to incline our ears to all of God's Word and let it be the final authority in our lives. God's Word is God Himself speaking to us. And the Word plainly reveals God's will, including His will to heal sickness and disease.

Some people read God's Word and still miss the fact that Jesus is the Healer. They ask, "If Jesus is the Healer and the Word is life and health to all our flesh, where does sickness and disease come from?" They think that if they're sick, *God* must have put sickness on them because He's trying to teach them something.

But if you'll get into the Word, the Holy Ghost will illuminate your mind and your spirit, and you will see that God is the Healer. Satan is the defiler — the one who tries to hurt people with sickness and disease. Satan is the author of sickness and disease, not God.

JOHN 10:10

10 The thief cometh not, but for to steal, and to kill, and to destroy: I am come that they might have life, and that they might have it more abundantly.

Remember, the Bible says that Satan is the thief that steals, kills, and destroys. And when Satan is finally eliminated from the earth — from all human contact —there will be nothing that will hurt or destroy (Isa. 65:25). So we know that anything that hurts or destroys is of Satan, not God. Sickness hurts and destroys, but God *heals* sickness. He doesn't *put* sickness *on* folks.

I've seen people get attacked by sickness and disease and say, "Well, God must have put this on me for some purpose. He probably has some great, mystical purpose in mind." Bless their darling hearts. But folks who believe this way are playing right into the devil's hands. They are being robbed of the blessings of healing and health that God wants them to enjoy.

It stands to reason that healing must be God's will or He wouldn't have given us instructions in Proverbs 4:20-22 to tell us how to experience life and health in our bodies.

People who don't believe it is God's will to heal have a distorted mental picture of the character of God. And the only way they can remedy that is to incline their ears to God's Word. If they would listen to what the Word says, they'd get the right picture of God in their hearts and minds, and their spiritual viewpoint wouldn't be distorted.

Light and Life

PROVERBS 4:20-22

20 My son, attend to my words; incline thine ear unto my sayings.
21 Let them not depart from thine eyes; keep them in the midst of thine heart.
22 For they are life unto those that find them, and health to all their flesh.

I get more thrilled teaching healing from Proverbs 4:20-22 than I do from any other standpoint, because this is the way I was healed and raised up from a deathbed as a teenager. I had a deformed heart and an incurable blood disease from birth. I never ran and played as a child like the other little children did. I used to just sit inside and watch from the window in awe as other children ran and laughed and played outside. I didn't have a normal childhood.

I know what it's like to have no hope for a better tomorrow. Five medical doctors told me I had to die because medical science couldn't do a thing for me. And I know what people who are dealing with sickness and disease in their bodies are going through, because I've experienced that too.

While sickness and disease ravaged my body, I would just stare at the ceiling hour after hour, day after day, wishing more than anything else just to be able to live. I agonized as I searched my mind for answers. I knew there had to be an answer somewhere.

I remember those days when the sun was shining brightly outside, but the room where I was imprisoned by sickness and disease seemed to be filled with darkness and death. Gloom hung like a shadow over me as I lay there on my sickbed and planned my own funeral. I was only a teenager. I hadn't even begun to live, yet medical science said I had to die.

But, glory to God, I also remember when the light of God's Word came shining in! The Psalmist said, *"The entrance of thy words giveth LIGHT; it giveth understanding unto the simple"* (Ps. 119:130). I couldn't even understand the Bible, but I kept reading it because I knew my answer was somewhere in God's Word.

MARK 11:24
24 Therefore I [Jesus] **say unto you, What things soever ye desire, when ye pray, believe that ye receive them, and ye shall have them.**

I had read Mark 11:24 before, but I didn't know what it meant or how to act on it. In the nighttime as I lay dying, I would repeat that verse over and over again all night long. I did that thousands of times.

At first Mark 11:24 was just words to me, but some way or another I knew there was healing for me in that verse. Finally, the light shone through, and the truth of God's Word dawned on my heart. I received healing from the top of my head to the soles of my feet. I got up off that bed of sickness completely well — and I've been well ever since!

"Yes, Brother Hagin," someone said, "that happened because God called you to preach."

But Mark 11:24 didn't work for me because God called me to preach. It worked for me because I inclined my ear to God's sayings. And it will work for you, too, if you will put God's Word first above every situation and circumstance that comes your way.

If you're struggling today with the tests and trials of life, stop your struggling and start inclining! Put God's Word first, and you will live the abundant life!

Memory Text:
"The thief cometh not, but for to steal, and to kill, and to destroy: I am come that they might have life, and that they might have it more abundantly."
— John 10:10

Roadblocks to Healing (Part 1)

Bible Texts: Hebrews 2:14; Matthew 8:17

Central Truth: God's Word reveals and thwarts the tactics Satan uses to keep you off the road to healing.

The road to divine healing is seldom an expressway. More often than not, it is strewn with roadblocks placed in our way by the devil to keep us from the blessing of health that God has provided.

These roadblocks wear subtle disguises and come from many sources. Some have their basis in tradition, others in superstition. Still others are based on misquoted and misunderstood scriptures.

This two-part lesson examines the seven most common roadblocks to divine healing that the believer must understand in order to remove them from his life.

Roadblock No. 1: 'God Sends Sickness Upon People'

Some have said that the Old Testament declares that God sent sickness upon people. Those who say this usually quote Exodus 15:26, *". . . If thou wilt diligently hearken to the voice of the Lord thy God, and wilt do that which is right in his sight, and wilt give ear to his commandments, and keep all his statutes, I will put none of these diseases upon thee, which I have brought upon the Egyptians: for I am the Lord that healeth thee."*

Similar scriptures are Isaiah 45:7, *"I form the light, and create darkness: I make peace, and create evil: I the Lord do all these things,"* and Micah 1:12, *"For the inhabitant of Maroth waited carefully for good: but evil came down from the Lord unto the gate of Jerusalem."*

Obviously, these passages in the *King James Version* of the Bible do not give the true meaning of the original Hebrew, for we know that God doesn't create evil. Evil couldn't have come from Heaven, because there is no evil there. God only *permits* evil. He doesn't *create* it. Nor does He create sickness — He only permits it to come as a result of man's disobedience.

The key to these difficulties lies in the fact that the active verbs in the Hebrew have been translated in the causative sense, when they should have been translated in the permissive sense.

Dr. Robert Young, the author of *Young's Analytical Concordance to the Bible* and an outstanding Hebrew scholar, points this out in his book *Hints and Helps to Bible Interpretation*. He says that in Exodus 15:26, the literal Hebrew reads: "... I will permit to be put upon thee none of these diseases which I permitted to be brought upon the Egyptians, for I am the Lord that healeth thee."

We must bear in mind Acts 10:38: *"How God anointed Jesus of Nazareth with the Holy Ghost and with power: who went about DOING GOOD, and HEALING all that were oppressed of the devil; for God was with him."* This important scripture shows that Jesus is the Healer and that Satan is the oppressor. *Nowhere in the entire Bible do we find God putting sickness on anyone!*

Remember that when God commanded Moses to go down into Egypt and lead the children of Israel out of bondage, He sent Moses to plead with Pharaoh to release the people. God didn't *want* the plagues to come upon the Egyptian people. But when Pharaoh hardened his heart, God withdrew His protecting hand and permitted the plagues to sweep over the land of Egypt.

When the final plague — death, the messenger of hell — was permitted, death went forth and destroyed the firstborn of every Egyptian household. Only then was Pharaoh compelled to yield and let the children of Israel go.

Where did the plague of death come from? Did it come from Heaven? Are there any dead in Heaven? The answer to these questions is no, of course. Death has never entered there, and it will never enter there. There will be no death in Heaven (Rev. 21:4)!

God is not the author of death; He's the author of life. God hates death. Where does death come from, then? It comes from Satan, who has the power of death.

HEBREWS 2:14
14 Forasmuch then as the children are partakers of flesh and blood, he [Jesus] also himself likewise took part of the same; that through death

he might destroy him that had the power of death, that is, the devil.

You see, the law of sin and death is the *devil's* law. But the law of the spirit of life in Christ Jesus is *God's* law. Romans 8:2 says, *"For the law of the Spirit of life in Christ Jesus hath made me free from the law of sin and death."* Death is our final enemy. And we have the promise that when Jesus comes again, this last enemy shall be put underfoot (1 Cor. 15:26).

Christ came to destroy "him that had the power of death" (Heb. 2:14). Satan isn't destroyed yet, but he will be put in the bottomless pit for a thousand years after Jesus returns. After the end of all things, Satan will be put in the lake of fire and brimstone forever (Rev. 20:10).

So the plague of death that came upon Egypt did not come until God withdrew His hand of protection and permitted it. His permission, however, should not be confused with commission. For example, God *permits* people to establish bars and nightclubs. He *permits* people to steal and kill. But He certainly doesn't *commission* those actions. There is a vast difference between *permission* and *commission*.

Now on the Day of Pentecost, Peter declared that Christ was crucified by the hands of wicked men: *"Him* [Jesus]. . . *ye have taken, and by wicked hands have crucified and slain"* (Acts 2:23). In other words, it was the devil's work done by his own children.

When the Pharisees stirred up the high priesthood against Jesus, He said, *"Ye are of your father the devil, and the lusts of your father ye will do. . ."* (John 8:44). It was not the work of God that the Pharisees turned people against Jesus, even though God permitted it.

But the fact that God permits wickedness doesn't mean that people have to commit sinful acts, any more than it means that people have to turn against Christ. Many people are crucifying Jesus afresh today because they are rejecting Him. Yet God doesn't commission them to reject Him; He just permits them to make their own choice — He gave man the free will to accept or reject His Son.

Roadblock No. 2: 'My Healing May Not Be God's Will'

When some people pray for healing, they think they should pray, "If it be Thy will." That prayer, however, is unnecessary, because God has plainly told us in His Word that it is His will to heal us.

A sinner wouldn't pray, "Lord, save me, *if* it be Thy will." That kind of prayer would be ridiculous, because God's Word declares that He is "... *not willing that any should perish, but that all should come to repentance*" (2 Peter 3:9). God's Word also states that "... *whosoever will, let him take the water of life freely*" (Rev. 22:17). Therefore, the sinner doesn't have to pray "*If* it be Thy will."

Similarly, it is just as ridiculous for a child of God to pray, "Lord, *heal* me, if it be Thy will." Why? Because the Bible tells us that Jesus already paid the price for our healing!

MATTHEW 8:17
17 That it might be fulfilled which was spoken by Esaias the prophet, saying, Himself took our infirmities, and bare our sicknesses.

When I read this verse and fully understood what it really meant, I rejoiced in it, for then I was able to emphasize the word "our." He took *our* infirmities and bore *our* sicknesses — and I am included in that word "our." Therefore, I can say that He took *my* infirmities and bore *my* sicknesses.

That brings it right down to where I live! In other words, I don't have to bear my sicknesses anymore, because *Jesus* bore them that I might be free!

When I made this discovery, I decided there wasn't any need for both Jesus *and* me to bear my

sicknesses. And if Jesus bore them that I might be free, why should I pray, "if it be Thy will"? The Bible states that it *is* His will!

Most people who don't believe in divine healing stay away from Matthew 8:17. However, occasionally a brave soul will come up with what he thinks is the answer to this scripture once and for all.

One person said this verse meant that Christ took the sicknesses of the people who lived at that time, but it doesn't apply to us today. But he forgot that Matthew wrote his Gospel *after* Jesus died. If healing had applied only to those living while Jesus was on this earth in the flesh, Matthew would have written, "He Himself took *their* infirmities and bare *their* sicknesses." However, Matthew didn't write it that way. The Holy Spirit, through Matthew, wrote, "He Himself took *our* infirmities and bare *our* sicknesses."

Someone else advanced the theory that this particular verse doesn't refer to the past, but refers to the future; therefore, it will come to pass during the Millennium. That can't be true, however, because there will be no need for healing then. Why? Because the curse will be lifted!

Paul said we will all be changed, "...*in a moment, in the twinkling of an eye ...*" (1 Cor. 15:52). Our bodies won't be plagued with sickness during the Millennium, so we will not need this provision for healing then.

No, the promise of divine healing belongs to us *now* — because we are subject to sickness in this life, not in the life that is to come. The promise that Jesus Christ took our infirmities and bore our sicknesses belongs to us today. Therefore, we don't need to pray, "If it be Thy will." God's Word has clearly shown us His will.

Still, someone else might ask, without quoting the entire verse, "But didn't Christ teach us to pray in Matthew 6:10, 'Father, Thy will be done'?" However, to use just one portion of that scripture is to use only half a truth. And as someone else said, "Beware of the half-truth. You may have gotten the wrong half!"

Christ taught us to pray, "Thy will be done in earth *as it is in Heaven.*" You see, He was teaching us to pray that God's will might be done here on earth just as it is done in Heaven. There is no sickness or disease in Heaven. So if it's not His will that there be sickness and disease in Heaven, then it's not His will that there be sickness and disease on earth. If His will is truly done on earth as it is done in Heaven, there will be no sickness or disease among us.

A man once told me he knew it wasn't God's will to heal a certain condition in his body because of an experience he had. He explained saying, just as he awoke one morning, his room lit up and someone in a long white robe appeared to him. He thought it was Jesus, although he did not see the person's face. The person said to him, "It is not my will to heal you," and then he disappeared. Ever since then, the man had accepted the idea that it wasn't God's will to heal him.

I asked him, "What if one of your unsaved loved ones told you that through a similar incident, God had revealed to him that it was not His will to save him? You would immediately point out scriptures to prove to him that it's not God's will for anyone to perish, but that all should come to repentance (2 Peter 3:9; John 3:16). You would explain that the person he mistook for Jesus was really a messenger of Satan, for Jesus wouldn't contradict His own Word, would He?"

I tell you, we can be just as certain that divine healing is God's will as we are that saving the lost is His will. And we know it by knowing His Word. God's Word is His will.

The same Bible that gives us John 3:16 also says, "*Surely he hath borne our griefs* [sicknesses], *and carried our sorrows* [diseases]: *yet we did esteem him stricken, smitten of God, and afflicted. But he was wounded for OUR transgressions, he was bruised for OUR iniquities: the chastisement of OUR peace was upon him; and with his stripes WE ARE HEALED"* (Isa. 53:4,5).

The Bible also says that Jesus *"... bare our sins in his own body on the tree, that we, being dead to sins, should live unto righteousness: by whose stripes ye were healed"* (1 Peter 2:24).

That's good news! Jesus Christ is the same yesterday, today, and forever (Heb. 13:8). He never changes. He can and *will* make believers whole today!

Memory Text:
"... I am the Lord that healeth thee."
— Exod. 15:26

Roadblocks to Healing (Part 2)

Bible Texts: Isaiah 38:1-5; 2 Timothy 4:20; 2 Corinthians 12:7-10

Central Truth: Removing the hindrances to healing puts the believer on the road to divine health.

The previous lesson covered two of the most common roadblocks to healing. In this lesson we will deal with five more roadblocks the devil uses to try to keep people from enjoying their God-given right to divine healing and health.

Roadblock No. 3: 'Hezekiah Used a Poultice'

ISAIAH 38:1-5

1 In those days was Hezekiah sick unto death. And Isaiah the prophet the son of Amoz came unto him, and said unto him, Thus saith the Lord, Set thine house in order: for thou shalt die, and not live.
2 Then Hezekiah turned his face toward the wall, and prayed unto the Lord,
3 And said, Remember now, O Lord, I beseech thee, how I have walked before thee in truth and with a perfect heart, and have done that which is good in thy sight. And Hezekiah wept sore.
4 Then came the word of the Lord to Isaiah, saying,
5 Go, and say to Hezekiah, Thus saith the Lord, the God of David thy father, I have heard thy prayer, I have seen thy tears: behold, I will add unto thy days fifteen years.

We read later in verses 20 and 21 that Hezekiah said: *"The Lord was ready to save me: therefore we will sing my songs to the stringed instruments all the days of our life in the house of the Lord. For Isaiah had said, Let them take a lump of figs, and lay it for a plaister upon the boil, and he shall recover."*

Some have wondered why God told Hezekiah to put a lump or poultice of figs on the boil. One very able

Bible scholar who was a medical doctor, minister, and Hebrew student says that according to the Hebrew translation, Hezekiah had a carbuncle on his neck, which can be very serious.

God already told Hezekiah that he would not die but would live for fifteen more years. Therefore, the poultice of figs was not necessary as a medicinal aid. It had no curative powers whatsoever. It served no medical purpose.

Many people through the years have used different poultices as cleansing agents, and some feel that Hezekiah's poultice may have been used in this manner. I am convinced, however, that God told Hezekiah to lay a lump of figs on the boil as an act of obedience and faith, just as He told Naaman the leper to dip in the Jordan River seven times so that his leprosy would be cleansed. Dipping in the muddy Jordan didn't have any curative value. It didn't heal Naaman any more than the poultice healed Hezekiah.

When the Spirit of God tells someone to do a certain thing, it usually involves an act of obedience to release that person's faith. That doesn't mean that everyone who does what the Lord tells a certain person to do will be healed. But it does mean that if God says for you to do something and you act upon it, you will be healed.

Roadblock No. 4: 'Paul Left Trophimus Sick at Miletum'

2 TIMOTHY 4:20
20 Erastus abode at Corinth: but Trophimus have I [Paul] left at Miletum sick.

Some quoting this verse argue that divine healing must not always be God's will since Paul left Trophimus sick at Miletum. But they fail to understand that Paul did not carry healing power around with him.

Healing is primarily a faith proposition on the part of the individual who receives. No matter how much faith a minister may have, the effects of an individual's doubt will nullify that minister's faith.

The Bible says, *"Can two walk together, except they be agreed?"* (Amos 3:3). And Jesus said in Matthew 18:19, ". . . *if two of you shall agree on earth as touching any thing that they shall ask, it shall be done for them of my Father which is in heaven."* (The negative side of this verse would be, of course, that if they don't agree, it won't be done.) So Trophimus' faith played a part in his healing.

In his writings, Paul differentiated between miracles and healing.

Miracles involving healing are instantaneous healings. Other healings are gradual, but they are still of God. For example, the Bible says that when Jesus prayed for the nobleman's son, the boy began to amend from that hour (John 4:46-53).

Often gradual healings are greater than instant healings, because some people who are healed quickly forget God. On the other hand, those who are healed gradually as they continue to believe God's Word often develop strong faith.

It may be that when Paul left Trophimus, Trophimus was still sick from all outward appearances, but the healing process had already begun. As I said earlier, healings can be gradual — but they are still of God.

Roadblock No. 5: 'Paul Had a Thorn in the Flesh'

2 CORINTHIANS 12:7-10

7 And lest I [Paul] should be exalted above measure through the abundance of the revelations, there was given to me a thorn in the flesh, the messenger of Satan to buffet me, lest I should be exalted above measure.
8 For this thing I besought the Lord thrice, that it might depart from me.
9 And he said unto me, My grace is sufficient for thee: for my strength is made perfect in weakness. Most gladly therefore will I rather glory in my infirmities, that the power of Christ may rest upon me.
10 Therefore I take pleasure in infirmities, in reproaches, in necessities, in persecutions, in distresses for Christ's sake: for when I am weak, then am I strong.

Because of this passage of Scripture, the thought is widely held that Paul had a sickness which God refused to heal. This teaching has led many to believe that it must be God's will for some of His saints to be sick, and it has held people in bondage when they should be delivered.

One common belief is that Paul suffered from some disease of the eyes and was nearly blind. The Bible states that the Lord Jesus appeared to Ananias in a vision and told him to go lay hands on Saul (Paul) that he might receive his sight. Ananias did, and God healed Saul (Acts 9:12-18). Therefore, to conclude that Paul had eye trouble because of that brief blindness would be to belittle the work of God.

Also, when Paul was on the island of Melita, he preached to the people and told them about the redemptive work of God. If his eyes had been full of pus, as some claim, would those people have believed God for healing? Yet the Bible says that when Paul laid hands on them, they were healed (Acts 28:8,9).

It is true that God permitted this "thorn in the flesh" to come upon Paul, but it was not from God. The scripture says that a "messenger of Satan was permitted to buffet him." *The Bible does not say that this thorn in the flesh was a sickness.*

Notice how the expression "thorn in the flesh" is used elsewhere in the Bible. Before the children of Israel went into Canaan's land, God told them to destroy the inhabitants of the country, the Canaanites. He said if they didn't destroy the Canaanites, it would cause them trouble in the future — the Canaanites would be a thorn in their side (Num. 33:55).

There was no reference to sickness in this scripture at all. Neither was Paul's thorn sickness. It was a messenger of Satan to buffet him. Everywhere Paul went, the devil stirred up strife against him.

Paul wrote of the many times he had been whipped and imprisoned. He was even stoned and left for dead. Yet in all of his writings about persecutions and tribulations, not once does he include sickness among them. Nowhere in the Scriptures do we find where Paul was ever disabled by sickness during his ministry.

Why, then, did God permit this thorn in the flesh to buffet Paul? The Scriptures say it was to keep Paul from developing a tendency to be prideful about the revelations and visions he'd had (2 Cor. 12:7).

Before anyone claims that he has a "thorn in the flesh," it might be well to ask how many revelations and visions he has had! Most people who think they have a thorn in the flesh haven't had any kind of revelation or vision. They're simply permitting Satan to defeat them and keep them from the blessings of God because of their ignorance and doubt.

However, there are some who do have a thorn in the flesh in some of the ways Paul did, because the devil is ever present to stir up trouble and hinder them in the work they are doing for God. But notice that God said, "*. . . My grace is sufficient for thee . . .*" (2 Cor. 12:9). Glory to God! *God's grace gives us power to rise above the buffetings of Satan.*

Roadblock No. 6: 'I'm Suffering For the Glory of God'

Those who support this belief usually point to the scripture in John chapter 9, when Jesus passed by a man who had been born blind.

Jesus' disciples asked Him who had sinned and caused the man to be blind — the man or his parents? Jesus said, "*. . . Neither hath this man sinned, nor his parents: but that THE WORKS OF GOD should be made manifest in him*" (v. 3).

Therefore, some people reason from this verse that the man was born blind in order that God might get glory from it. But Jesus went on to say, *"I must work the works of him that sent me, while it is day: the night cometh, when no man can work"* (v. 4).

Well, the works of God weren't made manifest in that blind man until Christ did what He was sent to do. Jesus healed the man's blindness. So "the works" that Jesus was referring to was *healing*, not the man's blindness.

What about Lazarus? Doesn't the Bible say he was sick for the glory of God? No, people just put their own interpretation on that. Remember when Jesus got word that Lazarus was sick? Jesus purposely tarried instead of hurrying to His friend's bedside. Then He told His disciples, *". . .This sickness is not unto death, but for the glory of God, that the Son of God might be glorified thereby"* (John 11:4).

Later when Jesus arrived in Bethany with His disciples, Lazarus had been dead four days. Lazarus' sister Martha told Jesus that if He had been there, her brother would not have died. Jesus answered, saying: *". . . I am the resurrection, and the life: he that believeth in me, though he were dead, yet shall he live: And whosoever liveth and*

believeth in me shall never die. Believest thou this?" (vv. 25,26).

Shortly after this, Martha protested Christ's command to roll away Lazarus' gravestone. She knew that after four days, his body would have already begun to decompose and stink. But notice Jesus' response: *". . . Said I not unto thee, that, if thou wouldest believe, thou shouldest see THE GLORY OF GOD?"* (v. 40).

Martha couldn't have seen the glory of God in her brother's death, because His glory hadn't been made manifest yet. The glory of God was manifested in Lazarus' resurrection and healing! (Lazarus not only had to be *resurrected*, but he also had to be *healed* of whatever had caused his death.)

God is glorified through healing and deliverance, not through sickness and suffering!

Roadblock No. 7: 'Sickness Is God's Chastening'

It is true that the Bible says, *"For whom the Lord loveth he chasteneth..."* (Heb. 12:6). However, it does not say, "Whom the Lord loveth He maketh sick!"

It is a mistake to take a small portion of Scripture and try to prove something. There is no reference to sickness in this text, and there is no implication of sickness or disease in the word "chasteneth" in the original Greek.

For the full meaning of this word we look to the writings of Dr. Robert Young, a recognized Greek scholar, and W. E. Vine, author of *An Expository Dictionary of New Testament Words*.

We learn from them that "chasten" literally means *to child train, educate, or teach*. Just as babies need to be taught and corrected so that they can grow to be healthy children and adults, baby Christians need to be taught and corrected so that they can grow to be spiritually healthy Christians. God's children need to be disciplined and governed, which is what this word means in the original Greek.

If *natural* children must be disciplined, corrected, and trained in love, we can expect God to train and discipline *us* with His hand of love, *"For whom the Lord loveth he chasteneth . . ."* (Heb. 12:6).

✳

Memory Text:

"And Jesus went forth, and saw a great multitude, and was moved with compassion toward them, and he healed their sick."
— Matt. 14:14

Spiritual Healing?

Bible Texts: Isaiah 53:4; 2 Corinthians 5:17;
Ezekiel 36:26; Mark 9:23; Matthew 9:27-30;
Mark 5:25-34; Matthew 8:5-10

Central Truth: When God heals, He heals
physically — but it's through the human spirit
or man's heart, where faith dwells.

Let's take another look at one of
our golden texts found in Isaiah 53.
It's a verse that should be familiar to
you since we've studied it in previous
lessons.

ISAIAH 53:4
4 Surely he [Jesus] **hath borne our
griefs, and carried our sorrows: yet
we did esteem him stricken, smitten
of God, and afflicted.**

Isaiah 53:4 says, *"Surely he hath
borne our GRIEFS, and carried our
SORROWS . . . ."* Again, this translation is from the *King James Version.*
But as the marginal notes in many
study Bibles point out, a more accu-
rate translation of the words "griefs"
and "sorrows" would have been "diseases" and "pains." So this verse actually reads: "Surely He — Jesus —

hath borne our *diseases* and carried
our *pains* . . . ."

This is the way Dr. Isaac Leeser
translated those two Hebrew words
for his Orthodox Jewish translation.
But you really wouldn't need to know
anything about Hebrew in order to
gain a clear understanding of what
this scripture meant, because you
could simply read what Matthew
said about Jesus, quoting Isaiah:
*". . . Himself took our INFIRMITIES,
and bare our SICKNESSES"* (Matt.
8:17).

Then in First Peter 2:24 we read,
"Who his own self [Jesus] *bare our
sins in his own body on the tree, that
we, being dead to sins, should live
unto righteousness: BY WHOSE
STRIPES YE WERE HEALED."*
Here Peter is looking back to the sac-
rifice of Christ when he says, "by

whose stripes ye were healed." Notice that "were healed" is past tense.

Now consider those last two scriptures together: "Himself took our infirmities and bare our sicknesses; by whose stripes ye were healed."

That verse in First Peter has been misunderstood by many in the past, so I want to look at it closely for a moment. I was reading after a supposedly outstanding Bible scholar who said, "First Peter 2:24 doesn't mean physical healing; it's referring to spiritual healing: 'By whose stripes you were healed *spiritually*.'"

Now this man was supposed to be a great authority on the Scriptures. But he must not have been reading the same Bible that I was reading. According to Second Corinthians 5:17, a sinner does not get healed spiritually.

2 CORINTHIANS 5:17
17 Therefore if any man be in Christ, he is a new creature: old things are passed away; behold, all things are become new.

The human spirit of the lost man or woman is not healed — it's *reborn*. The Bible says that once a person is in Christ Jesus, he becomes a *new* creature. Old things are passed away and all things become new. So First Peter 2:24 does not refer to spiritual healing.

Dispelling the 'Spiritual Healing' Myth

If you stop to think about it, there is no such thing as *spiritual healing* mentioned in the Bible. The concept of spiritual healing came into being when some psychologists got saved and filled with the Holy Spirit, and then they tried to mix psychology with the Word. They were born again and filled with the Spirit, all right — wonderful, sincere Christians — but they got confused.

You see, when your body gets healed, you are just healed of a sickness or disease. You don't get a brand-new body, do you? No, of course not. You still have the same body you had before you were healed.

Well, similarly, if your spirit were healed, you would still have the same spirit too. It would just be healed. But the Scriptures don't teach that at all. The Bible says that if any man is in Christ, he is a new creature (2 Cor. 5:17). Old things are passed away and, behold, all things become new — not half of them, *all* of them! So when you're born again, you're not the same spirit that you once were.

Notice what Ezekiel prophesied under the Old Covenant:

EZEKIEL 36:26
26 A new heart also will I give you, and a new spirit will I put within you: and I will take away the stony

heart out of your flesh, and I will give you an heart of flesh.

God was saying, "The time is coming when I'll establish the New Covenant, and I'll take out that old stony heart and put a new spirit within you. Then I'm going to put My Spirit in you."

That's why when I read where that fellow had said the Bible was referring to spiritual healing, I thought to myself, *Well, if that's the case, God made a mistake down there in Oklahoma!*

I mentioned in a previous lesson that during a meeting I held in Oklahoma years ago, a little 72-year-old woman was healed. The best doctors in the state said she would never walk another step the longest day she lived. She had been confined to a wheelchair for four long years.

When she was brought to my meeting, I just laid my Bible on her lap and had her read First Peter 2:24. And in ten minutes' time, she was jumping around, healed!

So if that verse meant spiritual healing, then God made a mistake. He ought to have healed her spiritually. But He healed her physically.

No, bless God, First Peter 2:24 means just what it says: "By whose stripes, ye were healed." That's talking about the healing of our human body, not our spirit!

There is only one sense in which divine healing could be called spiritual healing — if "spiritual" is being used to describe the work of God.

You see, in referring to divine healing, God is the One who heals your body, and He is a spirit (John 4:24). Therefore, in that sense you could say divine healing is spiritual healing. But that is not talking about the healing of the human spirit.

To put it another way, divine healing does not refer to being healed spiritually. However, it is spiritual because it refers to being healed *by the power of God.*

True Spiritual Healing

In ministering the tangible healing power of God, I have laid hands on people and felt the power of God go into them — then come right back out. Why? Because they didn't take hold of it!

This usually happens because folks are trying to receive healing with their mind. But divine healing is not mental. You can't contact God with your mind because He is not a mind. He is a spirit.

You see, when man heals (and man can heal, whether you realize it or not), he must either do it through the mind or through the physical senses. But when God comes on the scene as the Healer, He heals through the person's spirit.

Let me explain. God contacts us through our *spirit*, not through our mind or body — because, as we said, God is not a mind. Likewise, He is not a man (Num. 23:19). Although He has a spirit-body over in the spirit world — angels do too — God is not a *physical being*. He is a *spirit*. Therefore, He contacts us through our spirit, just as we contact Him through our spirit.

Now when God heals, He does heal *physically*, but it's through the human spirit. You see, God heals people through their faith — and the Bible says that faith is of the heart, the human spirit.

So divine healing is not mental as Christian Science, Unity, and other metaphysical teachers claim. Neither is it only physical as many in the medical world claim. It is spiritual — but only in the sense that it involves faith in the power of God as the *Word* proclaims.

I've seen it happen again and again: When people quit trying to contact God with their *mind* and believe they receive in their *heart*, they are healed instantly! You have to believe you receive the things of God by faith — and you believe with your heart (Rom. 10:10)!

With the *Heart* Man Believes

MARK 9:23
23 Jesus said unto him, If thou canst believe, all things are possible to him that believeth.

In chapter 9 of Mark's Gospel, a man came running up to Jesus, telling Him about his son who was possessed by a demon that would throw the boy into fire and water. The disciples had been unable to deliver the boy, so the father begged Jesus, saying, ". . .*if thou canst do any thing, have compassion on us, and help us*" (v. 22).

Jesus replied, ". . .*If thou canst BELIEVE, all things are possible to him that BELIEVETH*" (v. 23).

Notice that Jesus started working immediately on the man's believing, which had to do with his spirit. Jesus turned the father's plea for help around and said, "It's not a matter of what I can do. It's a matter of what you can believe: If thou canst *believe*, all things are possible!"

We see this same emphasis on faith repeated again and again in the ministry of Jesus. For example, read the following accounts of His healing the two blind men in Matthew 9, the woman with the issue of blood in Mark 5, and the centurion's servant in Matthew 8.

MATTHEW 9:27-30
27 And when Jesus departed thence, two blind men followed him, crying, and saying, Thou Son of David, have mercy on us.
28 And when he was come into the house, the blind men came to him: and Jesus saith unto them, Believe

ye that I am able to do this? They said unto him, Yea, Lord.

29 Then touched he their eyes, saying, ACCORDING TO YOUR FAITH be it unto you.

30 And their eyes were opened....

MARK 5:25-34

25 And a certain woman, which had an issue of blood twelve years,

26 And had suffered many things of many physicians, and had spent all that she had, and was nothing bettered, but rather grew worse,

27 When she had heard of Jesus, came in the press behind, and touched his garment.

28 For she said, If I may touch but his clothes, I shall be whole.

29 And straightway the fountain of her blood was dried up; and she felt in her body that she was healed of that plague.

30 And Jesus, immediately knowing in himself that virtue had gone out of him, turned him about in the press, and said, Who touched my clothes?

31 And his disciples said unto him, Thou seest the multitude thronging thee, and sayest thou, Who touched me?

32 And he looked round about to see her that had done this thing.

33 But the woman fearing and trembling, knowing what was done in her, came and fell down before him, and told him all the truth.

34 And he said unto her, Daughter, THY FAITH hath made thee whole; go in peace, and be whole of thy plague.

MATTHEW 8:5-10

5 And when Jesus was entered into Capernaum, there came unto him a centurion, beseeching him,

6 And saying, Lord, my servant lieth at home sick of the palsy, grievously tormented.

7 And Jesus saith unto him, I will come and heal him.

8 The centurion answered and said, Lord, I am not worthy that thou shouldest come under my roof: but speak the word only, and my servant shall be healed.

9 For I am a man under authority, having soldiers under me: and I say to this man, Go, and he goeth; and to another, Come, and he cometh; and to my servant, Do this, and he doeth it.

10 When Jesus heard it, he marvelled, and said to them that followed, Verily I say unto you, I have not found so great FAITH, no, not in Israel.

What do all these people have in common? They received God's provision of physical healing through their spirit, *because they believed with their heart!*

Memory Text:

"For with the heart man believeth unto righteousness; and with the mouth confession is made unto salvation."

— Rom. 10:10

Walk in the Light Of God's Word

Bible Texts: John 14:9; Psalm 107:20

Central Truth: Once we receive light from the Word concerning God's will to heal, He expects us to walk in that light.

I've said it before, but it bears repeating: *Jesus is the will of God in action! If you want to see God work, look at Jesus; if you want to hear God talk, listen to Jesus.*

JOHN 14:9
9 **Jesus saith unto him** [Philip] . . . **he that hath seen me hath seen the Father . . . .**

Well, what do we see Jesus doing in His earthly ministry? We see Him going about *doing good* and *healing* (Acts 10:38). So if Jesus is the will of God in action, then it must be the will of God to heal.

Healing was always in God's plan of redemption. For example, notice what the psalmist of old said in Psalm 107:

PSALM 107:20
20 **He sent his word, and healed them, and delivered them from their destructions.**

The word that God sent under the Old Covenant was spoken by the prophets. But the word that God sent under the New Covenant was the Lord Jesus Christ, the Word of God (John 1:1,14). God sent His Word — the Living Word — and healed us.

We're Already Healed!

God has given us the written Word so that we'll know what the Living Word has done for us. And we know that the Living Word healed us: He took our infirmities and bare our sicknesses; and by His stripes we *were* healed (Ps. 107:20; Matt. 8:17; 1 Peter 2:24).

Well, "were" is past tense. Therefore, in the mind of God, you're already healed! (You have to get your believing in the right tense for it to work for you!)

Now God will often let another person believe for you when you don't know the Word or you're still in the babyhood stage of Christianity. He will meet you on a lower level of faith.

But God expects mature believers to walk in the light of what they know. That's why it's the most difficult thing in the world for some Christians to get healed — because they already have light concerning healing, and God expects them to walk in that light, but they're not!

An Elder's Story

In September 1954, I was holding a three-week revival in a Foursquare church in California. The pastor's father-in-law would come regularly and sit in on the day services. He was an elderly gentleman — about eighty-two years old.

When we got over into the third week of the meeting, he came up to me after the morning service and asked, "Brother Hagin, may I speak to you?"

I said, "Yes." And he told me his story.

He said, "I came to California from Indiana in 1923. I had a physical condition that was terminal. The doctors told me that if I'd move out West where the winters weren't as severe, I might live another two years. So I packed up — lock, stock, and barrel — and moved my family to Los Angeles, California.

"That was the year Mrs. Aimee Semple McPherson built the 5,000-seat Angelus Temple in Los Angeles. Someone told me about her healing meetings and I went. Of course, I was desperate, because the doctors had said nothing more could be done for me.

"So I got in Mrs. McPherson's healing line and was healed by the power of God! Then I found out that I wasn't saved. I had always been a good church member, active in church work, and had just supposed that I already was a Christian. But I got saved and baptized with the Holy Ghost at her meeting too.

"I went to church there every week afterward and continued to hear the Word taught until we moved to northern California in 1933. Then in 1938 I developed a hernia. I said to my wife, 'I know all I have to do is have Mrs. McPherson lay hands on me, and that rupture will disappear.'

"While I was making plans to go to Los Angeles, I developed another rupture. Now I had a *double* hernia. When I did get back to the Angelus Temple, folks were beginning to come from everywhere for the daily healing meetings. It took me five days to get in the line, but finally Mrs. McPherson ministered to me — and I didn't get a thing!

'Aimee's Lost It'

"I thought, *Mrs. McPherson didn't have it tonight. If she had it like she did fifteen years ago, I would have gotten healed. But she didn't have it. So I'll just have to wait here until she gets it.*

"I stayed another five days with some kinfolks. That's how long it took me to get back in the healing line again. When she laid hands on me the second time, I didn't get a thing.

"My relatives asked me, 'Well, did you get healed?'

"I said, 'No. Whatever Mrs. McPherson had, she lost it. I went through her line twice. I guess she doesn't have it anymore.'

'The Evangelists Don't Have It Either'

"Brother Hagin, I carried my double hernia ten more years, from 1938 to 1948. Then while I was in the San Joaquin Valley, I happened to pick up a paper and noticed that some fellow was putting up a tent in Stockton. The ad said, 'Bring the blind, see the lame walk,' and so on. Well, all I had to do was get to Stockton!

"I went to this evangelist's meeting several times. He laid hands on me, but I didn't get a thing. I finally decided, *He doesn't have what he claims to have. If he had what Mrs. McPherson had — well, she had it, but she lost it — then I would have been healed!*

"Not too long after that, I saw in the paper that another fellow was holding a tent meeting in Sacramento. I knew all I had to do was get over to those meetings. So this other evangelist in Sacramento laid hands on me too, and I came away with both of my hernias. I said, '*He* doesn't have it either.'

Wasted Time

"I wound up going to several other meetings to be prayed for, and every time I'd go away saying, 'They don't have it!' Then last year in Santa Cruz, a famous prophet and evangelist was scheduled to preach at our church's campmeeting. I went to the meeting, got in his healing line, and without my ever telling him a word, he told me exactly what was wrong with me by the word of knowledge. But I didn't get healed.

"I went away once more saying, 'This brother doesn't have it. If he'd had what Mrs. McPherson had, I'd have gotten healed. Of course, *she* had it — but she lost it.'

"Then this year, Brother Hagin, *you* were advertised to preach at our campmeeting. I had heard about the vision you had of Jesus and how He appeared unto you, because it was published all through the church. I knew all I had to do was get to Santa Cruz and get in your healing line.

"I don't know how many times you laid hands on me in that campmeeting and later here in my son's church. But I wasn't healed. I said, 'I guess *Brother Hagin* doesn't have it. If he had what *Mrs. McPherson* had back in '23 — of course, now she's lost it — I'd have gotten healed.'"

Then this elderly man said to me, "But, you know, Brother Hagin, since I've been sitting here in these day services listening to you, I'm beginning to see something."

"What?" I asked.

"I'm beginning to see that God requires something of me."

I said, "Yes, brother. I don't mind telling you, you're wasting your time getting in healing lines. You've wasted thirty-one years in the Full Gospel church trying to get healed on someone else's faith. Why, instead of your having to be prayed for, you ought to be out praying for the sick yourself. No, brother, you're going to have to get healed on your own faith!"

You Have a Part To Play

You see, I was teaching on the subjects "How To Put Your Faith To Work" and "How To Confess With Your Mouth and Believe in Your Heart" in those daytime sessions. By sitting in on the services, that gentleman had begun to learn that *he* had a part to play.

That was in September 1954. In July 1955, ten months later, I went up to the Old Oak Ranch in the Sonora Mountains to preach for some Foursquare churches in that district. And one of the first fellows I saw was this elderly man. He was now eighty-three.

He waved at me from a distance and called, "Brother Hagin, Brother Hagin!" I waited for him to catch up with me.

Here he came running — at eighty-three! He threw his arms around me and hugged me. "Brother Hagin," he shouted, jumping up and down, "I'm completely healed! Both of my hernias have disappeared. I carried them around all those years, but now they're gone — and I got healed on my own faith!

"Not only that," he said, "but I'm doing just what you said. I'm eighty-three and retired, you know. So I'm out visiting the sick every day, praying for them and getting them healed!"

Praise God! That man was healed of his terminal illness back in 1923 through Aimee Semple McPherson's ministry because he was new in the faith. But years later when he developed those two hernias, something was required of *him*. God was requiring him to exercise his own faith.

You Have To Exercise Your Own Faith

When I minister healing, I lay hands on the sick in obedience to the spiritual law of "contact and transmission" — the contact of my hands transmits God's healing power into their bodies to undo that which Satan has wrought and to affect in them a healing and a cure (Mark 16:18; Acts 19:11,12).

Once I'm conscious that God's healing power has gone into them, I say, "There it is." That's as far as I can take people. That's where my responsibility ends and theirs begins.

You see, divine healing has to be appropriated by faith. You may be able to receive it through another person's faith for a while. But sooner or later you'll have to learn to exercise your own faith.

The Word of God is clear — God's will is healing. Now it's time to walk in the light of the Word you've received.

✳

Memory Text:
"Thy word is a lamp unto my feet, and a light unto my path."
— Ps. 119:105

ABOUT THE AUTHOR

Kenneth E. Hagin ministered for almost 70 years after God miraculously healed him of a deformed heart and an incurable blood disease at the age of 17. Even though Rev. Hagin went home to be with the Lord in 2003, the ministry he founded continues to bless multitudes around the globe.

Kenneth Hagin Ministry's radio program, *Faith Seminar of the Air*, is heard on more than 150 stations nationwide and on the Internet worldwide. Other outreaches include *The Word of Faith*, a free monthly magazine; crusades conducted throughout the nation; RHEMA Correspondence Bible School; RHEMA Bible Training Center; RHEMA Alumni Association; RHEMA Ministerial Association International; RHEMA Supportive Ministries Association; and a prison outreach.

God has a *specific* plan for your life.
Are you ready?
RHEMA Bible Training Center

"... Giving all *diligence*, add to your faith *virtue*,
to virtue *knowledge* ....
For if these things are yours and *abound*,
you will be neither barren nor *unfruitful*
in the knowledge of our Lord Jesus Christ."
—2 Peter 1:5,8 (*NKJV*)

∞ Take your place in the Body of Christ for the last great revival.
∞ Learn to rightly divide God's Word and to hear His voice clearly.
∞ Discover how to be a willing vessel for God's glory.
∞ Receive practical hands-on ministry training from experienced ministers.

*Qualified instructors are waiting to teach, train, and help **you** to fulfill your destiny!*

Call today for information or application material.
1-888-28-FAITH (1-888-283-2484)—Offer #4645
www.rbtc.org

– Notes –

– Notes –

— *Notes* —

– Notes –

– Notes –

— Notes —